NEW, REVISED EDITION

Preparing My Heart
for Easter

a Spiritual Pilgrimage
for the Easter Season

AMG
PUBLISHERS
ADVANCING THE MINISTRIES
OF THE GOSPEL

Ann Marie Stewart

Preparing My Heart for Easter:
A Woman's Journey to the Cross and Beyond

Original Edition © 2006 by Ann M. Stewart

Updated Edition © 2019 by Ann M. Stewart

Published by AMG Publishers. All Rights Reserved.

Updated Edition First Printing, 2019

ISBN 13: 978-1-61715-526-0

Cover artwork and design by Daryle Beam, Bright Boy Design, Chattanooga, TN

Editing and typesetting for this updated edition by Steele Editorial Services (https://steeleeditorialservices.myportfolio.com) with help from Linda Gilden

Original interior design by PerfecType, Nashville, TN

Printed in the United States of America

Dedicated to
my parents:
Bill and Ruth Roetcisoender

Acknowledgments

Thank you, Dad and Mom (Bill and Ruth Roetcisoender), for your continued support. I also thank Veronica Hall, who led a Bible study group and helped write the Guide for Leaders. A huge hug goes to the women who "test drove" an early model at Leesburg United Methodist Church: Kim Domin, Donna Fincher, Paulette Almond, Patti Henry, Shirley Bailey, Sarah Glaum, Marci Andrews, Kathi Pierce, Mary Frances Townsend, Jannine Vaughn; and to the women of the Edmonds, Washington test drive: Veronica Hall, Jennifer Sorensen, Michelle Hundthoft, Diana Young, Janet Wilkie, Joan Lundquist, Sherri Hamilton, Char Jacobson, and Beverly Heller. I thank on-line students Anne Miller, Nancy Fisler, Jodie Musgrove, Carrie Leslie, and Fern Tully; and heartfelt thanks go to the women at the Purcellville Baptist Women's Retreat, who gave my writing an audience.

For their faithful encouragement and prayers thanks go to Holly G. Coe, Carrie Leslie, Lydia and Milt Harris, Glenn and Helen Garner, Jane Eskew, Jill Dye, Leslie Williams, Barbara Boughton, Jodie Musgrove, Kim Domin, Marci Andrews, Joan McClenny, Anne Miller, Rachelle Knight, and Karen van der Riet.

For generous editing assistance I thank Michelle Albanese, who gently revealed what's a manageable length, along with Lydia Harris and Mary Kate White, and for their spiritual proofreading, Pastor Mike Emerson, and Rick Howe, Director of Dayspring Center for Christian Studies. For graphic and technical help thanks go to Sherrill Kraakmo, and Jannine Vaughn.

Thanks to AMG editors who believe in preparing hearts for holy days.

Most of all PRAISE BE to the One who made Easter a celebration!

About the Author

ANN MARIE STEWART is the Christy Award® winning author (Best Debut Novel, 2017) of *Stars in the Grass* (Shiloh Run Press). Previously she authored three Bible studies that helped establish the Preparing My Heart series (AMG Publishers). She also writes the column "Ann's Lovin' Ewe" for *The Country Register* and blogs for "Mentoring Moments."

When she's not writing, she's waving her arms directing musicals, teaching private voice, middle schoolers, or watching UVA Basketball or *Madam Secretary*. In her free time, she hangs out with her husband, raising two lovely daughters and a whole flock of fuzzy sheep on Skye Moor Farm, in Virginia—where unscripted drama provides plenty of entertaining material. For more information about Ann, you can read her blog "The Upside of the Story" at www.AnnMarieStewart.com.

Introduction

A thrill went through me when I saw Him enter the city gate riding on a donkey. His faraway gaze mystified me, and yet his warm smile of acknowledgment seemed so personal. "Hosanna!" we shouted.

His disciples echoed with, "Blessed is He who comes in the Name of the Lord!"

I wasn't prepared for the unified surge of excitement that rippled through the crowd. Children jumped up and down to get a better look; women waved their palm branches, and men hailed him. I was engulfed in the energy, enthusiasm, and excitement of the moment. When He reached out to the children crowding around Him, He looked so much like the Sunday school pictures of my childhood.

As an actor in our community passion play, I have experienced many emotions as I seek to understand the first Easter. My various roles as follower of Christ, Mary Magdalene, and Mother of Jesus have challenged me to look at Jesus from new perspectives.

But one problem is that I'm influenced by knowing the *end* of the story. What would it have been like to be a woman in the crowd during Jesus' day, experiencing great hope, and then great loss, not comprehending that He would return? Walt Wangerin writes in *Reliving the Passion,* that knowing the end of the story alters our experience of comprehending the final week.

> It is the experience of genuine grief that prepares for joy. . . . The disciples approached the Resurrection from their bereavement. For them the death was first, and the death was all. Easter, then, was an explosion of Newness, a marvelous splitting of heaven indeed. But for us, who return backward into the past, the Resurrection comes first, and through it we view a death which is, therefore, less consuming, less horrible, even less real. We miss the disciples' terrible, wonderful preparation." (p. 32)

How do *we* prepare ourselves for a *new* celebration of Easter? By looking at how Jesus elevated women. When I began researching *Preparing My Heart for Easter,* what struck me was the importance of *women* in the Easter story. Over and over I saw the phrase "the women" repeated.

The Women:
- traveled with Him and supported Him out of their own means (Luke 8:1–3)
- followed Him to the cross (Matthew 27:55–56; Mark 15:40–41)
- remained at the cross (Luke 23:48–49)
- saw the tomb and how His body was laid (Luke 23:55–56)
- prepared spices and returned to the tomb (Luke 24:1)
- first heard and told the Good News (Matthew 28:6–8)

- first saw the resurrected Jesus (Matthew 28:9; Mark 16:9)
- helped form the early church (Acts 1:14)

As I studied those scriptures, I had to ask, *Why were the women so devoted? Why were the women at every step of the journey?*

Discover the answers to these questions as we journey with Jesus and meet the women whose lives He touched. You may relate to someone whose life He changed and realize He can change your life, too. Our eyes will be fixed on Him. Then we will join the men and women who celebrated His resurrection and see how the early church begins as our own spiritual growth develops.

To assist your study, please cut out your own bookmarks and place them in Matthew, Mark, Luke, John, Psalms, and Isaiah to help you in your reading. When multiple references are listed, the ones in parenthesis are optional scriptures for further study. Or use online tools to help you locate the references more quickly. I can't encourage you enough to simplify the search on days with multiple references.

Meet Jesus in a new way this Easter season. As your relationship with Him grows, you'll never want to be without Him. Let's prepare for an Easter unlike any other, an "Explosion of Newness." Join me as we journey to Jerusalem.

Lest I forget Gethsemane, lest I forget Thine agony,
Lest I forget Thy love for me, lead me to Calvary.

"Lead Me to Calvary"
by Jennie Hussey and William Kirkpatrick

Contents

Acknowledgments   *v*

About the Author   *vi*

Introduction   *vii*

Week One—Preparing for the Journey: 3/3/20 Rachel
    What is Lent?   1

Week Two—Traveling with Jesus: 3/10/20 Marianne
    Four Women Touched by Him   18

Week Three—Traveling with Jesus: 3/17/20 Ruth
    Seven Women Who Met Jesus   35

Week Four—Traveling with Jesus: Kay 3/24
    Two More Women Touched by Him   54

Week Five—Passion Week: Entering Jerusalem Gwen 3/31   72

Week Six—Passion Week: The Last Days 4/7 Llewlee   89

Week Seven—The Way of Sorrow 4/14 Sandy   102

Week Eight—Where Do We Go from Here? 4/21 Judy   125

Guide for Leaders   *147*

WEEK ONE

Preparing for the Journey

What Is Lent?

Monday: Packing for the Trip
What Is Lent?

Welcome fellow traveler! I look forward to journeying with you all the way to the cross and beyond. The first week of study will equip us for the following seven as we learn about AD 30, the cultural attitudes of the day toward women, and the backgrounds of Easter terms.

In *Preparing My Heart for Advent: A Spiritual Pilgrimage for the Christmas Season* (Updated Edition, AMG Publishers, 2018), we prepared our hearts for the coming of Immanuel—*God with us.* In *Preparing My Heart for Easter* we will journey with *God with us* all the way to the cross and beyond as we learn of His death, resurrection, ascension, and the gift of the Holy Spirit.

Are you ready? You'll need your Bible, a pencil, a time and place to meet with God, and a commitment to journey with Him. The relationship you form with Jesus will *transform* your life.

Which sounds like you?

I sometimes feel like the sinner woman. I cannot look into Jesus' face.

I am like the widow at Nain. I am grieving, but Jesus is seeking me.

I am like the woman at the well. I'm staying away from crowds and not seeking Jesus.

I am like Simon Peter's mother-in-law. Others bring Jesus to me.

I am like Jairus' wife. Others reveal Jesus to my family and me.

I am like the woman in the crowd listening to Jesus' lessons.

I am like Martha. I fervently serve the Lord through my actions.

I am like the woman who followed Christ. I am desperately trying to grab the fringe of His garment.

> Where will you meet with Jesus each day?

I am pleading with God like the Canaanite woman over a finan-
cial situation or a family member's health.
I know I am a sinner and have felt Jesus' forgiveness. I love to
worship Him.
I am like Mary Magdalene. Jesus has so changed my life, I long to
be near and serve Him.
I am like Mary, Martha's sister. I love to sit at Christ's feet

As one of these women of AD 30, what would draw you to Jesus? What was so attractive and revolutionary about Him? According to Luke 8:1–3, the women followed him from one town and village to another, supporting His ministry from their own means. Historian Paul Maier, author of *In the Fullness of Time*, confirms the importance of women.

> Women play a more enviable role than men in the events of Holy Week. In contrast to the misunderstandings, betrayals, denials, and flight of the male followers of Jesus, it was women who anointed Jesus at Bethany, who punctured Peter's pretenses in the courtyard of Caiaphas, who warned Pilate to release Jesus because he was innocent, who commiserated Jesus' fate on the way to Golgotha, and who stood loyally under the cross until the end.[1]

📖 Read the passages below and note what might have caused His followers—especially women—to walk with Jesus. From each passage, list one central verse and one characteristic that might prompt you to follow Jesus.

Mark 6:30–44 *34 – Jesus saw the huge crowd as He stepped from the boat, & He had *(compassion) on them because they were like sheep without a shepherd. So He began teaching them many things.*

Mark 10:13–16 *v 15 ... anyone who doesn't *(receive the kingdom of God like a child) will never enter it.*

John 11:32–36 *35 ... Jesus wept. Jesus was not afraid to show His emotions. He cared. He weeps with us in our sorrow.*

Matthew 18:2–5 *4—So anyone who becomes a* (humble) *as this little child is the greatest in the* (kingdom) *of Heaven. And anyone who* (welcomes) *a little child like this on my behalf is welcoming me.*

Jesus' Words in Action: What did you learn about Jesus? How can you be more like Him today? What might cause you to join Him? Keep following! We have a wonderful journey ahead.

Tuesday: Tell Me the Stories of Jesus

My favorite line from the hymn "Tell Me the Story of Jesus" is "*Words full of kindness, deeds full of grace, all in the lovelight of Jesus' face.*" Today, can you sit in the "lovelight of Jesus' face?" Just what did that look like?.

Isaiah 53:2 says there wasn't anything handsome about Him, and New Testament scriptures seem to confirm this. Paul Maier writes,

> Jesus' physical appearance must have seemed very normal indeed—no towering figure, no nimbus, no halo. His enemies required the services of a Judas to point him out in the dusk of Jerusalem, Mary Magdalene mistook him for a gardener at the Easter tomb, and to the Emmaus disciples he looked like nothing more than a fellow traveler. [2]

His magnetism came from within. His *words* and *actions* attracted crowds. Paul Maier also describes what He was *not* as well as what He *was.* He was *not* an ascetic, legalist, intolerant person, or wimp. He *was* a friend, a caring healer, and a man who could enjoy a party. He socialized with sinners and publicans and was strong in body, mind, and purpose. [3]

Philip Yancey, author of *The Jesus I Never Knew*, states, "the Gospels present a man who has such charisma that people will sit three days straight, without food, just to hear his riveting words." He seems excitable, impulsively "moved with compassion" or "filled with pity." Yancey describes a man with a wide range of emotions: sympathy, exuberance, anger, and grief. [4] He was human and God.

> "He grew up before him like a tender shoot, and like a root out of dry ground. He had no beauty or majesty to attract us to him, nothing in his appearance that we should desire him." (Isaiah 53:2)

Jesus is also a great storyteller. Without a microphone, He keeps an audience of thousands riveted. He knows their needs and engages his listeners with examples they can relate to. Let's pretend we're hearing these stories for the first time. What is it that encourages you to follow Him?

📖 Read Luke 15:1–24.

1. What three examples does Jesus use to illustrate the joy of a sinner being found? *V6... he calls friends & neighbors to celebrate with him b/c he found the lost sheep V9- lost coin- calls friends & neighbors to rejoice ③ V20- Prodigal son- ran to him, embraced & kissed him.*

> "And when he has found it, he lays it on his shoulders, rejoicing." (Luke 15:5)

Can you see the Good Shepherd's joy at finding His single lamb? He must rejoice knowing you are walking beside Him today.

But, knowing His audience, Jesus expands on the story to include a *woman* who has ten silver coins and loses one. This may equal a full day's wage. This tidy housekeeper lights a lamp, sweeps the house, and searches until the coin is found. These two stories lead into the story of the Prodigal Son. Three times Jesus shows us there is joy in heaven over the sinner who comes to know Jesus.

2. Why would Jesus tell this story three different ways? *So that the people could and identify & understand God's love for them*

3. What does this tell us about His audience? *They were lost without hope. He tells them that they are of great value. They were looking for a Savior.*

4. What does each story emphasize? *- They are valued by God - God has been searching/ pursuing them to bring them into the fold - He waits with love & compassion.*

Jesus wants the tax-gatherers and sinners to know, "There will be more joy in heaven over one sinner who repents, than over ninety-nine righteous persons who need no repentance" (Luke 15:7).

Jesus' Words in Action: Jesus reveals He has come to seek the lost. That encourages me! He loves even the lowliest. He doesn't favor kings and priests and extends his love to sinners and *nobodies.*

But when you give a banquet, invite the poor, the crippled, the lame, the blind, and you will be blessed. Although they cannot repay you, you will be repaid at the resurrection of the righteous. (Luke 14:13–14)

In what way can I be like Jesus and show love and attention to those who can never repay my kindness? *With unconditional love.*

Ash Wednesday: How Do We Celebrate the Good News?

> *In what way can I be like Jesus and show love and attention to those who can never repay my kindness?*

I saw my kindergartener's new piano teacher cross the parking lot with an ash mark across her forehead. I didn't want Julia to be scared or ask an inappropriate question, so I bent down and gave Julia a 10-second explanation of what little I knew of Ash Wednesday. Julia's response surprised me: "Can I do that next year, too, Mommy?"

Ash Wednesday is the seventh Wednesday or 46 days prior to Easter and marks the beginning of Lent which focuses on our need for forgiveness and salvation. Lent originated as *lencten* or "lenthen" of daylight to describe the lengthening of the days. Lent began in the second century as a way of educating new Christians for the forty days prior to their Easter baptism. (What a day to be baptized into the church!)

When we think of Lent, the following words come to mind: penitence, reflection, suffering, death and resurrection, prayer, fasting, discipline, study, contemplation, preparation, introspection, self-examination, repentance, and retreat.

The forty days of Lent begin with Ash Wednesday and end with the Great Vigil of Easter, subtracting all Sundays, which instead celebrate the resurrection. The number *forty* is representative of Jesus' forty days alone in the wilderness—His own spiritual journey.

You, too, can have forty days to prepare for Easter. This may mean turning *away* from certain sinful behaviors and returning *to* God

Why give up something for Lent? Perhaps it will help you share in His sufferings. Maybe the discipline will help you focus on Him. It may help you experience sorrow over your sin and what it cost the Messiah. It puts God first, not belongings, desires, or habits.

Or perhaps you want to add something for Lent. You could reconcile with a friend, reach out to a neighbor, read a Lenten devotional, or do this Lenten study.

Shrove Tuesday—The Tuesday preceding Ash Wednesday. Shrove means "to repent."

Shrovetide is the three days before Lent (Sunday, Monday, and Tuesday). These same three days are also called "Carnival" meaning "removal of meat," "Mardi Gras," or "Fat Tuesday," a very secular celebration of costumes, parades, dancing and drinking.[5]

Ash Wednesday—Throughout the Old Testament, ashes represent sorrow and remorse (Esther 4:1–3; Job 42:6; 2 Samuel 13:19). Wearing an ash smudge across the forehead began in the 12th century. Palm branches from the previous year were burned, their ashes mixed with oil, and then a cross was smudged across the Christian's forehead as a constant reminder that we are all sinners and desperately in need of forgiveness. But one pastor at my church, after the mark was placed on each participant's forehead, asked the parishioners to turn to their neighbors and wipe off the mark. The idea was to carry the mark *inwardly*.

In addition to Ash Wednesday and Lent, there are important events which occur to commemorate the last week of Jesus' life.

Palm Sunday celebrates the day Jesus entered Jerusalem on a donkey to loud shouts of "Hosanna!" Palm Sunday marks the beginning of Holy Week.

Passover commemorates Israel's freedom from Pharaoh. Although Egypt's firstborn males were killed during the tenth plague, the Israelites were saved by the mark of the blood of the lamb. Similarly, we are saved through the blood of Jesus, the Lamb of God.

Feast of Unleavened Bread is a seven-day Jewish festival following Passover in which no leavening products are used. This festival commemorates the Israelites' hasty flight from Egypt and their arrival to safety.

"The Great Three Days"—*Triduum*

1. Maundy Thursday is the Thursday prior to Easter. Maundy is Latin for *mandatum novum* or "new commandment" remembering Jesus' new commandment recorded in

> "Come to me, all you who are weary and burdened, and I will give you rest. Take my yoke upon you and learn from me, for I am gentle and humble in heart, and you will find rest for your souls. For my yoke is easy and my burden is light." (Matthew 11:28–30)

John 13:34. "A new command I give you: Love one another. As I have loved you, so you must love one another." Thursday services remember Jesus' betrayal, the Lord's Supper, His washing the disciples' feet, and His final teachings as recorded in John's Gospel.

2. Good Friday may be an alteration of the term "God's Friday." Good Friday remembers Jesus' crucifixion and His last words from the cross (John 18:1—19:37). On Good Friday a Tenebrae (Latin—*shadows* or *darkness*) service features scriptures, meditations, and extinguished candles as the Christ candle exits the room.[6]

Great Vigil is Holy Saturday or Black Saturday, remembering the dark moments before the resurrection.

3. Easter celebrates Jesus' resurrection from the dead.

Ascension recognizes Jesus' return to heaven, which occurred forty days after Jesus' resurrection.

Pentecost celebrates the gift of the Holy Spirit and is celebrated fifty (pente) days after Passover. It also correlates with the Jewish Festival of the Feast of Weeks, falling seven weeks after the harvest.

The Calendar

Why does Easter move each year? The date is determined by a complicated timetable involving the first full moon and the vernal equinox, making Easter fall sometime between March 22 and April 25. If you're confused about how it's determined, join the centuries of individuals who have tried to find a system for the entire world to celebrate Easter on the same Sunday!

For your *personal* celebration, below are some ideas others have used during Lent.

Celebrate Lent with...

Easter Devotional. Read *Journey to the Cross* by Helen Haidle with your children.

Amon's Adventure by Paul Ytreeide. A daily reading covering the story of a little boy during the time of Christ.

Resurrection Eggs. These eggs for children can be ordered from FamilyLife.com. As an accompaniment, read *Benjamin's Box, A Resurrection Story*.

Lenten Wreath. This is the Advent candle wreath in reverse. Instead of lighting a new candle each of the four

Sundays prior to Christmas, on each of the seven Sundays of Lent, you extinguish one of the seven candles until you are left with no candles on Good Friday. Incorporate scripture reading as you extinguish the candles. Re-light all the candles on Easter, for Jesus conquers the darkness![7]

Plan a Walk to observe the signs of spring and creation. Notice the light and joy in the new changes. "For since the creation of the world God's invisible qualities—his eternal power and divine nature—have been clearly seen, being understood from what has been made, so that men are without excuse" (Romans 1:20).

Stations of the Cross. Though begun by early Christians retracing Jesus' steps to Golgotha, both Catholics and Protestants still set apart a time and place to meditate, worship, and give thanks at a series of stations which focus on Christ's journey to the cross.[8]

Memorize one verse each week.

Focus on one of Jesus' seven "I AM" statements each Sunday. When Jesus explains He is the **I AM** of the Old Testament, He connects the God of the Old Testament with the Messiah of the New Testament.

The Great I AM

In Exodus 3:1–18, we find Moses tending the sheep, Speaking through a burning bush that isn't being consumed, God instructs Moses to speak to Pharaoh, but Moses questions God: "Who am I, that I should go to Pharaoh and bring the Israelites out of Egypt?" God reassures Moses He will be with Him. But Moses questions further, "What if they ask your name? Then what should I say?"

God said to Moses, "I AM WHO I AM. And God further expounds, "This is my name forever, the name by which I am to be remembered from generation to generation" (Exodus 3:15).

I AM is God's name forever. When Jesus says I AM, He's saying He is the God of the past, the God of the present, and

---

The Colors of Lent

Red	*Blood of Christ*
Black	*Sin — Good Friday*
Grey	*Ashes—Ash Wednesday (sorrow)*
Purple	*Royalty—King Jesus*

Can we ever truly understand His suffering and what He did for us? Probably not. But oh, how we need to grasp our need for a Savior!

the God of the future. He is the God who will save the people from their oppression and persecution and deliver them to a land of milk and honey.

That is why I AM is so profoundly powerful.

You cannot read the words I AM without understanding both Old and New Testament implications. Let's look where Jesus made I AM claims.

"Then Jesus declared, '**I am** the bread of life. He who comes to me will never go hungry, and he who believes in me will never be thirsty.'" (John 6:35)

"**I am** the living bread that came down from heaven. If anyone eats of this bread, he will live forever. This bread is my flesh, which I will give for the life of the world." (John 6:51)

1. Because Jesus is the Great I AM and the _bread of life_, I will _never_ _hunger_.

After each claim, fill in what I AM means to *you*, just like in the sample above.

"When Jesus spoke again to the people, he said, '**I am** the light of the world. Whoever follows me will never walk in darkness, but will have the light of life.'" (John 8:12) *gate*

2. Because Jesus is the great I AM and the *master of my soul*, I will *worship only him. Find redemption in Him*

"Therefore Jesus said again, 'I tell you the truth, **I am** the gate for the sheep." (John 10:7)

"**I am** the gate; whoever enters through me will be saved. He will come in and go out, and find pasture." (John 10:9)

3. Because Jesus is the great I AM and the *Shepherd of His Sheep*, I can enter and *know God*.

"**I am** the good shepherd. The good shepherd lays down his life for the sheep." (John 10:11)

"I am the good shepherd; I know my sheep and my sheep know me— just as the Father knows me and I know the Father—and I lay down my life for the sheep." (John 10:14–15)

4. Because Jesus is the great I AM and the *resurrection & life*, He will *rise* and I will *have life*.

"Jesus said to her, '**I am** the resurrection and the life. He who believes in me will live, even though he dies.'" (John 11:25)

5. Because Jesus is the great I AM and the *truth and the life*, I will *come to God through Jesus*

"Jesus answered, '**I am** the way and the truth and the life. No one comes to the Father except through me.' " (John 14:6)

6. Because Jesus is the Great I AM and the *true vine* and the *gardner* and the *branches*, I can *bear much fruit*.

"**I am** the true vine, and my Father is the gardener." (John 15:1)

"**I am** the vine; you are the branches. If a man remains in me and I in him, he will bear much fruit; apart from me you can do nothing." (John 15:5)

7. Because Jesus is the great I AM and the *Alpha & Omega*, through Him I will *live eternally with Him*.

In Revelation, we see additional I AMs.

"**I am** the Alpha and the Omega, the First and the Last, the Beginning and the End." (Revelation 22:13)

"I, Jesus, have sent my angel to give you this testimony for the churches. **I am** the Root and the Offspring of David, and the bright Morning Star." (Revelation 22:16)

Jesus' Words in Action: Most of the time when I'm stressed out, it's because *I am* focusing on *myself.* My sentences begin with *I am* instead of claiming promises and proclaiming the power of the *great* I Am.

Lent encourages us to focus on Jesus. In obedience to His teaching, how can you "fast" from doing something or how can you add something that causes you to focus on the great I AM and what He did for you?

Walter Wangerin explains,

> …when we genuinely remember the death we deserve to die, we will be moved to remember the death the Lord in fact did die—because his took the place of ours. Ah, children, we will yearn to hear the Gospel story again and again, ever seeing therein our death in his, and rejoicing that we will therefore know a rising like his as well.[9]

I AM the

Bread of Life

Light of the World

Gate (Door) for the Sheep

Good Shepherd

Resurrection and the Life

Way, Truth, Life

True Vine

Thursday: Join Jesus on the Mountain

Wouldn't it be great to hear Jesus give a sermon? We can! We can listen to the Sermon on the Mount and learn what was important to Him. If you have time, read Matthew 5-7; today we'll focus on a few topics.

📖 Read Matthew 5:3–11 below and read and "hear" (as if for the first time) what Jesus taught both men and women.

Matthew 5:3–11, New International Version (NIV)

3"Blessed are the poor in spirit, *They know they need God.*
   for theirs is the kingdom of heaven.
4Blessed are those who mourn,
   for they will be comforted.
5Blessed are the meek,
   for they will inherit the earth.
6Blessed are those who hunger and thirst for righteousness,
   for they will be filled.
7Blessed are the merciful,
   for they will be shown mercy.
8Blessed are the pure in heart,
   for they will see God.
9Blessed are the peacemakers,
   for they will be called children of God.
10Blessed are those who are persecuted because of righteousness, for theirs is the kingdom of heaven.
11"Blessed are you when people insult you, persecute you and falsely say all kinds of evil against you because of me.

1. In the scripture passage above, circle each occurrence of the word "who" and then underline the blessing related to that "who." Then draw an arrow connecting the two, as seen in the example drawn in verse 3.

2. Star which "blessed" encourages you today.

3. What title would you give that sermon topic? *Blessed/Happy are those who follow Christ's teachings. Keep our eyes on Jesus.*

📖 Skipping farther down, read Matthew 5:43–45.

Matthew 5:43–45, New International Version (NIV)

43"You have heard that it was said, 'Love your neighbor and hate your enemy.' 44But I tell you, love your enemies and pray for those who persecute you, 45that you may be children of your Father in heaven. He causes his sun to rise on the evil and the good, and sends rain on the righteous and the unrighteous.

> "The Spirit of the Sovereign LORD is on me, because the LORD has anointed me to preach good news to the poor. He has sent me to bind up the brokenhearted, to proclaim freedom for the captives and release from darkness for the prisoners, to proclaim the year of the LORD's favor…"

4. What is new and different about Jesus' teaching? "But I tell you…"

love your enemies & pray for those who persecute you.

📖 Read on in Matthew 6:25–34.

5. List what Jesus cautions us *not* to worry about (verses 25, 31).

About everyday life; food/drink, clothes; material things.

6. What is the ultimate solution to worrying (verse 33)? *Seek the Kingdom of God above all else, & live righteously, & He will give you everything you need.*

What reassurance! We women are always planning, considering, and wondering, but Jesus gave a simple solution to those kinds of needless cares: Seek first His kingdom.

📖 Read Matthew 7:7–11.

Matthew 7:7–11, New International Version (NIV)

7"Ask and it will be given to you; seek and you will find; knock and the door will be opened to you. 8For everyone who asks receives; the one who seeks finds; and to the one who knocks, the door will be opened.

9"Which of you, if your son asks for bread, will give him a stone? 10Or if he asks for a fish, will give him a snake? 11If you, then, though you are evil, know how to give good gifts to your children, how much more will your Father in heaven give good gifts to those who ask him!"

7. What is the result of each action?

Ask = *receive*

Seek = *find*

Knock = *the door will be opened.*

8. What might this sermon be entitled? *Be persistent in seeking God's guidance.*

Jesus' Words in Action: What did you learn about Jesus? What qualities in Jesus draw you near to Him? Since His words are so beautiful and He loves us, how can we share His love and teaching with others? How can *His* story be our story? *Jesus wants to give us good things as we grow closer to Him.*

Friday: Why Did They Want a King? Why Did They *Need* a Savior?

The Jews of Matthew, Mark, Luke, and John were waiting for religious and political freedom. Their wait had been long. Your Bible, with its sliver-thin pages, reveals no gap between the Old and New Testaments. However, there are four hundred years of waiting. There was little to write, because the people weren't listening, and God wasn't speaking through the prophets.

1. Look at the map of Palestine on the following page. Let's focus primarily on Judea, Samaria, and Galilee.

You'll note that Rome is not on the map; it's too far away. And yet Rome is the long-distance governing power. This creates political problems and control issues. Rome is added to the long series of oppressive governments.

During the Intertestamental Period, the Jews were under the thumbs of four successive empires. The Maccabees at last gave the Jews a short period of independence. However, Roman occupation followed in 63 BC and on into the first century. Is it any wonder the Jews wanted their independence and freedom?

Politically

Rome appointed certain rulers to represent the Jews. King Herod the Great ruled at the time of Jesus' birth. When Herod died, he divided his region among his sons, none of whom respected the Jews. Questioning the rulers resulted in death. Herod's son, Herod Antipas, ruled during Jesus' time

Palestine in the Time of Jesus

in Jerusalem. He was more interested in political power than Jewish faith. Herod Antipas had to keep peace at all costs.

Spiritually

Chief Priests/Sadducees tended to be worldly and tempted to compromise to position themselves well with the Romans.

John the Baptist warned the Pharisees and Sadducees to produce fruit in keeping with repentance (Matthew 3:8) and that "The ax is already at the root of the trees, and every tree that does not produce good fruit will be cut down and thrown into the fire" (Matthew 3:10). But the religious leaders did not want someone marching into Jerusalem and causing such a disturbance that they would lose what little power they had.

Though the Jews wanted a powerful political leader who would represent them, they really needed a spiritual king: Jesus of Nazareth.

Let's look at Jesus at the point when He announces He is the One prophesied in the Old Testament.

When Jesus first begins His ministry, Jesus, The *Word made flesh* holds the *Word of God*. Jesus unrolls a scroll of Scripture and reads from the first two verses of Isaiah 61.

📖 Read Luke 4:16–30.

2. Because the Spirit of the Lord is upon Him, what does this passage tell us Jesus has the power to do (verses 18–19)? *Bring Good News to the poor; to proclaim that Captives will be released; The blind will see; the oppressed of the set free; the Tx of Lord's favor has come.*

Jesus returns the scroll and sits down. The eyes of everyone in the synagogue are fastened on Jesus (Luke 4:20). Wouldn't you have loved to be there for that scene? There must have been a hushed moment of anticipation.[10]

And then He completes the teaching by adding the crux of the message, "Today this scripture is fulfilled in your hearing" (Luke 4:21). So far He has merely read the Word. Now He reveals that He *is* the Word.

3. What are some of their initial reactions (verse 22)? *Everyone spoke well of Him & His gracious words*

4. What other proverb does Jesus quote in response (verse 23)? *Physician, heal yourself - meaning, "Do miracles here in your hometown.*

5. What does Jesus claim they will ask of Him (verse 23)? *Perform miracle.*

Jesus then recalls Old Testament incidents where healing came to *one* instead of *many*. This incites Jesus' listeners to drive Him out of town and attempt to throw Him off the cliff. What a terrible way to end synagogue for the day!

6. Why did Jesus' words infuriate them?

He was telling them that He was/is the Messiah + that He would perform miracles as a way of gaining acceptance.

Luke 4:30 says that Jesus walks right through the crowd and continues on His way. Jesus will do that. He knows His time, His mission, and His purpose. He knows that in Nazareth, the people lack faith and so He will not exercise His power in Nazareth as He did in Capernaum.

Jesus' purpose was determined before the beginning of time, before the creation of the world, and before man ever sinned. In other words, God planned salvation before there was time. Read the scriptures below to note how early our grace was promised.

"This grace was given us in Christ Jesus *before the beginning of time.*" (2 Timothy 1:9)

"He was chosen before the creation of the world, but was revealed in these last times for your sake." (1 Peter 1:20)

". . . a faith and knowledge resting on the hope of eternal life, which God, who does not lie, promised before the beginning of time." (Titus 1:2)

The Messiah came to take away our sins, to bind and heal our wounds, and make us inwardly clean so that we may serve Him with a clear conscience. That's the kind of King we all need.

Jesus' Words in Action: How can we let Jesus bind our broken hearts and set us free?

Accept the salvation He so freely offers.

Works Cited

1. Maier, Paul L., *In the Fullness of Time: A Historian Looks at Christmas, Easter, and the Early Church* (Grand Rapids, MI: Kregel, 1991), 182.

2. Ibid., 91.

3. Ibid., 91, 93.

4. Yancey, Philip, *The Jesus I Never Knew* (Grand Rapids, MI: Zondervan, 1995), 88.

5. Dennis Bratcher, "The Season of Lent," http://www.cresourcei.org.

6. Bratcher, "The Days of Holy Week," http://www.cresourcei.org.

7. Noel Piper, "The Light Shines in Darkness," Proverbs 31 Woman, March 2005.

8. Bratcher, "The Cross as a Journey," http://www.cresourcei.org.

9. Wangerin, Walter Jr., *Reliving the Passion: Meditations on the Suffering Death and Resurrection of Jesus as Recorded in Mark* (Grand Rapids, MI: Zondervan, 1992), 22.

10. Ray Vander Laan and Focus on the Family Video (That the World May Know Series), *Faith Lessons on the Life and Ministry of the Messiah: The Rabbi* (Grand Rapids, MI: Zondervan, 1996, 1998), Volume 3, Video 2.

Traveling with Jesus

Four Women Touched by Him

Monday: What Was It Like to Be a Woman in AD 30?

Women's lives have changed significantly over the last 2000 years. To understand how Jesus appeared to the women of his time and to know why Jesus seemed so radical and liberating, we must travel back to the first century and see Jesus anew. Set your Bible aside and enjoy the information that will place you back in the first century.

Clothing

As a woman you wear a linen petticoat (*kolbu*) as well as a dress (*Baldinajja linene*). A robe is tied over this (*Istomukhvia*) and a scarf wrapped around your waist (*Pirzomata*). You also wear a girdle the colors of your tribe's stripes. A scarf hides your face.[1]

Social Interactions

As you move about, you are not to talk to men. The Jewish writings of the *Talmud* and *Mishna,* as well as the religious leaders, discourage men from speaking to women because it might be misinterpreted or lead to adultery.[2]

Philip Yancey writes,

> In social life, few women would talk to men outside of their families, and a woman was to touch no man but her spouse. Yet Jesus associated freely with women and taught some as his disciples. A Samaritan woman who had been through five husbands, Jesus tapped to lead a spiritual revival (notably, he began the conversation by asking **her** for help). A prostitute's anointing, he accepted with gratitude. Women traveled with his band of followers, no doubt stirring up much gossip. Women populated Jesus' parables and illustrations, and frequently he did miracles on their behalf.[3]

In other words, Jesus violates the rules, treating women as equals, something unheard of during that time.[4]

Education

If you feel shunned socially, it continues into the classroom. Your education includes religion, reading, and writing. A boy or man's education continues longer than a girl's.[5]

Religious Education and Practice

You have had limited religious teaching and practice. The Torah is for men; the spindle for women.[6] It is a patriarchal society where men hold the power in politics as well as religion.

The religious "Supreme Court" or Sanhedrin is a men-only club. They alone can wear scriptures on their foreheads. The temple was also a men-only club except for the women's court. Women *can* worship by doing good works. The women *can* prepare for the Sabbath by cooking three kosher meals, filling lamps, filling jugs with water, cleaning the house, washing laundry.[8] But there is plenty they *cannot* do.

Number of Times Men and Women are Mentioned in the Gospels	
Daughters—24	Sons—327
Mothers—72	Fathers—293
Woman/women—78	Man/men—295[7]

Women were not permitted to pray, in public or at home. In the synagogue they were set apart from the men, hidden behind a screen. They couldn't bear legal witness, nor did their presence in the assembly count toward a quorum. Not to mention the fact that rabbis did not speak to women in public.[9]

Jesus changed this. Yancey writes, "To take just one example of the revolutionary changes Jesus set in motion, consider Jesus' attitude toward women. In those days, at every synagogue service Jewish men pray, 'Blessed art thou, O Lord, who hast not made me a woman.'"[10]

Romans responsible for end of polygamy

But when Mary sits listening at Jesus' feet, there is no rebuke. Jesus applauds her and says she has chosen the good part. Jesus actually encourages women to follow, listen, and grow spiritually.[11]

Laws of Purity

For men, not only is it, "Don't talk to a woman in public," but also, "Don't touch." If you as a woman are considered unclean, you can make others unclean. What makes you unclean? Menstruation is one thing. Your impurity lasts seven days, during which anything you sit on or lay down on is considered unclean. Anyone touching your bed or anything you sit on has to wash his or her clothes and take a bath. A man who has relations with you will be considered unclean for seven more days, and his bed is considered unclean, too! (Leviticus 15:19–24).

Rabbis encourage safety, and so they have added days before and after the seven, warning of the possibility of death from contamination.[12]

Childbirth also makes you ceremonially unclean for seven days following the birth. You aren't purified for another thirty-three days after that. You can't go into the sanctuary or touch anything sacred until that time is over. That's if you have a boy. But if you give birth to a girl, the period of uncleanness was *twice* the length (Leviticus 12:1–8).

But Jesus touched women. And when a bleeding and thus "unclean" woman touched *Him*, He recognized her faith and did not rebuke her (Mark 5:25–34).[13]

He is more interested in the women's faith, and He is more concerned about what is on the *inside* than the *outside*, the spiritual rather than the physical.[14] Jesus knows evil comes from the inside out (Mark 7:21–23). What comes from a person's heart is what makes *him* unclean.

Yancey describes how sickeningly radical Jesus appeared to the Pharisees. He was out to change the system and liberate the unclean.

> In the midst of this religious caste system, Jesus appeared. To the Pharisees' dismay he had no qualms about socializing with children or sinners or even Samaritans. He touched, or was touched by, the "unclean": those with leprosy, the deformed, a hemorrhaging woman, the lunatic and possessed.[15]

Legal

Legally, women have fewer rights, decisions, and little power. You can't own land, and you are not a valid witness in court. A widow cannot inherit; the money stays in her husband's family, and she is at their mercy for her care. If you are unmarried when your parents die, the inheritance goes to your brother.

When Jesus arrives, He is concerned for the widows. His half-brother went on to write, "Religion that God our Father accepts as pure and faultless is this: to look after orphans and widows in their distress and to keep oneself from being polluted by the world" (James 1:27).

In Old Testament writings, females did not hold the same financial value as males. A male (age 20–60) dedicated to the Lord was worth fifty shekels of silver whereas a female was worth thirty (Leviticus 27:1–5). Children were worth less than that. But followers of Jesus went on to write, "There is neither Jew nor Greek, slave nor free, male nor female, for you are all one in Christ Jesus" (Galatians 3:28).

Jesus values the women and children even though Gospel writers don't count them in the feeding of the thousands and turned the children away (Matthew 14:21, 15:38; Mark 10:14–15).[16] Similarly, Jesus does not show partiality in His treatment. Jesus heals and teaches both men and women. "Jesus' actions, when contrasted with the dictums of the rabbis, makes it clear that Christ's coming introduces a redemptive process designed to lift and restore women to the position they enjoyed in original creation."[17]

> " 'Who are my mother and my brothers?' he asked. Then he looked at those seated in a circle around him and said, 'Here are my mother and my brothers!' " (Mark 3:34–35)

The Family

While motherhood is beautiful, Jesus emphasizes that the blessedness was not in the suckling of a child but in being in the family of God, comforted by God, hearing God's Word, and obeying it (Luke 11:27–28).[18]

> "As Jesus was saying these things, a woman in the crowd called out, 'Blessed is the mother who gave you birth and nursed you.' He replied, "Blessed rather are those who hear the word of God and obey it" (Luke 11:27–28).

With Jesus, once again, the status of the heart is more important than family structure and marital status. Similarly, he reveals that His family members are those who do His Father's will. He begins bringing equality to family roles.[19]

Marriage and Divorce

Married women have few marital rights and are vulnerable to divorce for invalid reasons, depending on who is interpreting the law. It is less probable that a woman could start divorce proceedings. In AD 30, a husband can just say, "You are divorced," but at least the Jews require a certificate to obtain a legal divorce.[20]

> "He answered, 'Anyone who divorces his wife and marries another woman commits adultery against her. And if she divorces her husband and marries another man, she commits adultery.' "
> (Mark 10:11–12)

Jesus reminds listeners that divorce is also an issue of the heart, a hard one, and not a part of God's created plan. God created male and female to unite and become one flesh. "Therefore what God has joined together, let man not separate" (Mark 10:5–9).

He warns that getting a divorce is more than just handing out a certificate and notes that *both* parties have equal responsibility in the marriage.[21]

Country/City

The rules are stricter for a woman of Jerusalem than for a woman in the country. The wealthy Sadducees exert a great deal of control over the temple and possess a significant amount of money; whereas the priests in more rural areas are as poor as the fishermen, artisans, shopkeepers, and farmers they serve. The wives also might have worked to sell their husband's produce. Author Sue Richards sums up today's lesson well,

> Women, who ever since the Fall had taken a lowly place in human society and even in Israel's faith, are lifted up and given striking prominence by Jesus Christ. Christ consistently displayed a concern for women that contrasts sharply with the way women were viewed and treated in first-century Jewish society.[22]

As you can see, Jesus changes women's lives for the better. From Christ's genealogy to His birth and then to His interaction with others, women take on important roles. Jesus' genealogy includes five women: Rahab (prostitute), Tamar (had sex with father-in-law), Ruth (Moabitess), the wife of Uriah (had adulterous relationship with King David), and Mary the mother of Jesus (poor young peasant girl).

God sent His only Son to be born of a *female*. "But when the time had fully come, God sent his Son, born of a woman, born under law" (Galatians 4:4). God transformed the lives of those in the genealogy as well as the lives of all women.

Though it might appear that women are in the *background* in the first century, it's just that the lights haven't been turned up on their part of the stage. I am moved by how Jesus cares for women, and I delight in flooding the stage to highlight Jesus' transformative power in our lives.

Jot down any information you remember next to the list of women below. If there are lots of blanks, good! Then the study for the next two weeks will seem new and fresh!

New Testament Women

Jairus' daughter and wife

Hemorrhaging woman (How would you like to be remembered for *that*?)

Syrophoenecian woman

Mary Magdalene

Peter's mother-in-law

Woman at the well

Mary/Martha

Adulterous woman (A name worse than *hemorrhaging!*)

Bent, crippled woman

Widow at Nain

Anointing woman

Salome

Jesus' Words in Action: As Jesus interacted with women, He affirmed their value, challenged their faith, and broke society's rules.[23] Jesus wants us to sit at His feet and listen to His teaching? How has Jesus changed your life, and how can He further transform you?

Tuesday: Jesus Heals Peter's Mother-in-Law

Our bags are packed with background material to help us get to know the many women we'll meet. First we'll meet Simon Peter's mother-in-law.

The setting is the Sabbath. Look back at your map from Week One (page 14). Peter's mother-in-law lives in Capernaum, a city on the Sea of Galilee. This city buzzes with activity because it's on the caravan route to Damascus and is a customs station and Roman garrison.

📖 Read Luke 4:38–39; Mark 1:29–34 (also Matthew 8:14–15).

Place a bookmark at Luke 4 and Mark 1.

Sometimes Jesus heals "long-distance," and sometimes He heals "up close and personal." Matthew 8:15 says that Jesus touched Peter's mother-in-law's hand. I find myself jealous. How comforting to slip one's hand in the Savior's and find healing!

1. How soon is Peter's mother-in-law healed (Mark 1:31; Luke 4:39)? *As Jesus took her hand.*

When I recover from a fever, it's a slow return to normalcy. Gradually I can eat food and begin to tackle the housework. I don't look my best after sweating for days, so, if the "whole town" gathered at my door after my near-death experience, I wouldn't be *thrilled to death* to entertain (Mark 1:33)!

2. Yet, through the power of Jesus, what does this woman do (Luke 4:39)? *She gets up & prepares a meal for them.*

The King James Version says, "immediately she arose and ministered unto them." What a beautiful description of thankful service.

3. How do you think Peter's mother-in-law felt about the work of her son-in-law after she was healed? *transformed. Jesus touched her to heal her. He showed genuine concern for her.*

"Surely he took up our infirmities and carried our sorrows, yet we considered him stricken by God." (Isaiah 53:4) ✢

4. If you were one of the many men and women outside the door, what do you think your thoughts about this Healer and Teacher would be? *They were probably amazed that he touched a woman & spoke to her.*

5. Even before the sun sets, what follows this very personal healing (Luke 4:40)? *Crowds brought their sick to be healed & He cast out their demons.*

Mark adds more details about the discipline of Jesus. After the whole town has gathered at Peter's mother-in-law's door and Jesus has healed diseases and driven out demons, Mark adds, "Very early in the morning, while it was still dark, Jesus got up, left the house and went off to a solitary place, where he prayed" (Mark 1:35).

Once Jesus' followers catch up and let Him know everyone is looking for Him, Jesus responds, "Let us go somewhere else—to the nearby villages—so I can preach there also. That is why I have come" (Mark 1:38). Yes, He came to heal, but He has a message to preach. And to successfully prepare for His mission, He needs time alone with the Father.

Jesus' Words in Action: We need time alone with the father, too. What better way to begin a day than to imitate Jesus' priorities. Even if you can't pray or study for hours during this Lenten season, try to spend the first waking moments giving praise and thanksgiving to God.

In the morning, O LORD, you hear my voice; *in the morning* I lay my requests before you and wait in expectation." (Psalm 5:3)

"But I will sing of your strength, *in the morning* I will sing of your love; for you are my fortress, my refuge in times of trouble." (Psalm 59:16)

"But I cry to you for help, O LORD; *in the morning* my prayer comes before you." (Psalm 88:13)

"Satisfy us *in the morning* with your unfailing love, that we may sing for joy and be glad all our days." (Psalm 90:14)

Wednesday: No Accidental Encounter with the Woman at the Well

Have you ever felt you just don't belong? Or perhaps you wonder if your past precludes you from fitting in with other Christians. A look at Jesus' genealogy reveals He descended from a line of imperfect individuals. Jesus came to earth and reached out to the poor, sick, sinners, and, in today's example, someone who doesn't even reach out to Him.

Samaritans were despised. The feud between Jews and Samaritans dates back more than seven hundred years before Jesus was born and had to do with intermarriage, deportation, and resettlement (2 Kings 17:3–24). Pure Jews hated these new converts and the defilement of their race and religion.[24]

Samaritans were so despised that Jewish travelers would go *around* Samaria rather than *through* it. Pharisees considered contact with Samaritans contaminating.[25]

But Jesus doesn't believe in *going around* Samaria or going down the *other side* of the street to avoid someone. He makes that very clear when an expert of the law asks Him, "*Who is my neighbor?*" and Jesus tells the following story of "The Good Samaritan," a term that could be considered oxymoronic in that time.

As the story goes, robbers attack a traveler and leave him stripped and beaten on the road. A priest and Levite pass him by on the *other side* of the road. But the Samaritan takes pity on the man, dresses his wounds, brings him to an inn, and pays for his recovery. The merciful Samaritan is considered the *neighbor, the hero,* in contrast to the religious leaders, who walk past the injured man (Luke 10:27–37).

Jesus' stories and His actions reveal He is breaking down walls of prejudice and hatred. Jesus has come for all. The *Samaritan woman* at the well could have been a woman to avoid. But Jesus, who dines with tax collectors and sinners, doesn't operate that way.

📖 Read John 4:4–30

The Samaritan woman probably feels ostracized from her community. Rather than coming to the well in the cool morning hours when other women would enjoy socializing, she arrives during the sixth hour, which could be noon (Jewish time) or more likely six o'clock in the evening (Roman time).[26] At this hour she expects to be alone.

> "If you knew the gift of God and who it is that asks you for a drink, you would have asked him and he would have given you living water." (John 4:10)

Earlier, Jesus had left Judea and journeyed twenty miles in the heat and dust back to Galilee,[27] and He deliberately did not go down the *other side* of the road. Instead of avoiding Samaria, He went straight through it to the heart of the village of Sychar to meet someone whose life He planned to change.

Their conversation needs subtitles beneath to explain the language barrier. The Samaritan woman is talking about H_2O, and He is talking about the *living water* of salvation.

1. Who initiates the discussion? Considering what you know about the relationship between men and women, why is this unusual (verse 7)?

Jesus initiates

2. What surprises the woman about Jesus' request (verse 9)?

That He would speak to her.

Because she is a Samaritan, a Jew would not have shared utensils with her.[28] But Jesus' dialogue continues on another level. He has asked for H_2O from a deep well, but it is the woman herself who needs living water.

3. What is the "*gift of God*" (verse 10)?

Living water flows; it is pure and drinkable as opposed to dead water in cisterns made by man. To enter the synagogue, a Jew would wash in *living water* to be purified. When we're dry and thirsty, it is only the Living Water of Jesus that can cleanse and fulfill us.[29]

4. What does Jesus say about Living Water? Fill in the blanks from John 4:13–14.

"_____ who drinks this water will be thirsty again, but whoever drinks the water I give him will _____ thirst. Indeed, the water I give him will become in him a _____ of water welling up to_____ _____." (John 4:13–14)

The words *everyone* and *never* are strong. She wants that *living water.* That's when Jesus shifts gears and suddenly tells her to call her husband and return. When she responds that she doesn't have a husband, she is being truthful to a degree. She's had *five* husbands, and the man she's with currently is *not* her husband. Jesus knows more than any stranger *should* know about her. With that kind of knowledge, He has to be a prophet! She then talks about one of the differences in the Samaritan and Jewish faiths—where God is worshiped.

But Jesus explains, *where* He is worshipped is not the point. Differences in ethnicity would no longer divide. Jesus

> "Yet a time is coming and has now come when the true worshipers will worship the Father in spirit and truth, for they are the kind of worshipers the Father seeks." (John 4:23)

[Handwritten at top: Spirit is opposite of anything earthly. This is the new covenant.]

explains, we need to worship in spirit and in truth. What does *spirit and truth* mean? Are we *true* worshipers, or are we stuck in subtleties that divide believers? Are we the kind of worshipers the Father seeks?

The Samaritan woman then remarks that the Messiah will come. Jesus' answers, "I who speak to you am he." Right here Jesus claims to be the great "I AM" from Exodus 3:14, which we studied in Week One.

5. And while we eagerly await the woman's response, what happens (v. 27)?

6. What are the disciples surprised to find and why would John record what they did not ask?

7. Who might have been the silent observer and recorder of the previous, seemingly private conversation?[30]

[Handwritten: John and/or Holy Spirit.]

> "He chose the lowly things of this world and the despised things—and the things that are not—to nullify the things that are, so that no one may boast before him."
> (1 Corinthians 1:28–29)

The woman who wouldn't draw water with a crowd races into town proclaiming, "Come, see a man who told me everything I ever did. Could this be the Christ?" (John 4:29). Her encounter with Jesus has transformed her. This has been a great counseling session. Someone knew her story and background and loved her anyway!

📖 Read John 4:39-42 for the rest of the story.

8. As a result of the woman's testimony, what three things happen (v. 30, 39-42). *[Handwritten: She believed, testified, encouraged others to follow him.]*

9.Perhaps the most profound result is in v. 42. Fill in the blanks: "We no longer _____ just because of what ___ said; now we have heard for ourselves, and we _____ that this man really is the _____ _____ ___ _____" (John 4:42).

What a glorious finale! "We know that this man really is the Savior of the world." What if our words inspired others to seek out the Savior?

In His encounter with the Samaritan woman, Jesus broke racial, social, cultural, and religious rules. He shouldn't have spoken to a Samaritan woman alone, and certainly not about religious topics.[31] And yet in this encounter, Jesus took that which was despised and weak and used it to bring wisdom to others, and the Samaritan woman becomes one of the first missionaries in the Gospels!

Jesus' Words in Action: What did you learn about Jesus today? In what way does Jesus seek us out? In what ways are you surprised that He knows so much more about you? How is this almost reassuring? Does that make it easier to talk to Him today?

Thursday: Throwing Stones

People in glass houses shouldn't throw stones. We've all heard that saying and know it means others may attack us if we attack them. Another well-known quote is, "If any one of you is without sin, let him be the first to throw a stone. . ." (John 8:7).

Stoning was the punishment for adultery. The woman of John 8 was caught in the act of adultery, and she would pay the price.

📖 Read John 7:53—8:11 to learn more about throwing stones.

In this passage, Jesus spends time before dawn on the Mount of Olives.

1. What might he have been doing?

2. You've seen how Jesus treated the Samaritan woman. How is Jesus' response to the Pharisees and teachers of the law different (verses 3–5)?

The adultery concern levied by the Pharisees is sexist: only one partner is brought in. For the woman to have been caught in the act may mean the event is a setup.[32] If she were a known prostitute, that would not have been difficult. But the purpose of bringing her to the *temple* is to trap Jesus.

3. Consider what Jesus draws on the ground in verse 6. What do you think he writes? *Maybe writing specific sins of those around.*

> "If any one of you is without sin, let him be the first to throw a stone at her." (John 8:7b)

4. What kind of questions do you think the Pharisees ask (verse 7)?

5. How does his audible response apply to the times you might accuse, condemn or gossip about another person?

6. After Jesus resumes his writing, what happens to the accusers?

7. What might Jesus have written on the ground?

8. What does Jesus say to the crowd. "Let _____ _____ of you who is _____ sin be the _____ to _____ a stone at _____.

9. Jesus continues writing and the crowd scatters. Why? *They were just as guilty.*

Jesus and the woman are alone, and Jesus asks where they are and has anyone condemned her to which she answers "No one, sir,"

Jesus' next words are so important.

10. Fill in the following blanks from v. 11. Then _____ do I _____ you. ____ _____ and _____ your life of _____.

> "For God did not send his Son into the world to condemn the world, but to save the world through him." (John 3:17)

Jesus' Words in Action: We memorize John 3:16 but what about the verse that follows? *"For God did not send his Son into the world to condemn the world, but to save the world through him."* (John 3:17).

Jesus sends the adulterous woman out with a command to "Go now and leave your life of sin" (verse 11).

I cannot imagine this woman returning to her former life after being *saved* by the Messiah.

If you can relate to this woman and are looking for a fresh start, Jesus gives you the inspiration to step out and claim it. He wants this woman—and all of us—to begin again. Believe in Him, accept Him as your Savior, and ask for forgiveness. Find a non-pharisaical church that can embrace and disciple a new believer. Go now and leave your sin. Become a new creation in Christ! (2 Corinthians 5:17).

Note: Some scholars doubt whether John wrote John 7:53—8:11. Early manuscripts do not include this passage or place it in other locations.

> "For God so loved the world that he gave his one and only Son, that whoever believes in him shall not perish but have eternal life." (John 3:16)

Friday: The Widow at Nain

Do you ever wonder if your heart catches Jesus's attention? Now let's meet the widow of Nain and see how much Jesus cares.

Read Luke 7:11–17 (the widow at Nain).

Place yourself again in AD 30. As a woman of that time, you may have heard that Jesus heals. You may have heard the Samaritan woman at the well explain that Jesus is the Messiah. But today, for the first time, Jesus reveals His power over death.

Jesus leaves Capernaum and encounters a lowly widow in the village of Nain, ten miles from his native Nazareth (Refer to map on page 14). Jesus' large crowd meets the widow's large crowd to make quite a gathering of witnesses. Quite a busy intersection!

1. What three facts do you know about the woman Jesus meets (verse 12)? *Widow, one son, husband died, no one to support her.*

2. How does Jesus react to her (verse 13)?

If Jesus said to me, "Don't cry" (Luke 7:13), I'd probably cry harder. There are times I'm barely holding it together and then someone lovingly says, "I care." Compassion, sympathy, and empathy bring me to tears. Oh, the sadness of that poor, lonely widow who has lost her only son. Luke is the only Gospel writer who records this scene. Do you wonder why?

She now has no provider or companion. All hope must be lost except for the arrival of a man whose heart goes out to her. Can she comprehend how dearly He loves her? Can she fathom how deeply He wants her to have life and to have it abundantly?

Jesus meets us at the gate, too. When all hope is lost, He sees our troubles, and He does care. He'll meet you anywhere, and He'll hear our cries.

How do you suppose the crowds react? The men carrying the coffin have stopped their progress. Jesus' words are to the point, "Young man, I say to you, get up!" (Luke 7:14). Does that sound ridiculous? Jesus talking to a dead man? But what happens? The dead man (Note: *dead* man) sits up and talks. He doesn't mumble or cough; he *talks*. *1st raising of a dead man.*

3. What do you suppose the "dead man" says?

Probably did't know he died? Maybe not.

4. Who do you suppose the "dead man" sees surrounding him? What do their faces look like?

Amazed

Two separate crowds of men and women watch as Jesus gives "him back to his mother." What a gift! She may not even have asked Him for this, but Jesus knows her need, he understands her sorrow, and grieves to the point of responding to her pain.

This is one of the few instances of Jesus raising someone from the dead. We will see the raising of Jairus' daughter, and later Lazarus. But this is the first recorded time that Jesus resurrects a person from the dead.

> "He threw himself at Jesus' feet and thanked him—and he was a Samaritan." (Luke 17:16)

5. What is the crowd's reaction (verse 16)?

6. Who do they claim Jesus is (verse 16)?

They even explain, "God has come to help his people" (verse 16). Indeed. But did any of them really understand that He truly is more than a prophet? Can they fathom that Jesus is "God with us," Immanuel? Do the disciples even grasp that this man is really *God on earth* to help his people?

7. What is the ultimate consequence of this resurrection (verse 17)? *Jesus applied*.

A friend of mine suddenly lost her four-year-old daughter to Strep A virus. There was nothing Lori or the doctors could have done to save little Katie. As her daughter was ushered into heaven, Lori came to know Jesus Christ as her savior. She compares herself with the widow of Nain. "My first instinct wasn't to begin crying out to God—I didn't really know Him at that time. He saw *me* and had compassion!" Jesus met her at the gate with His presence and peace. As Lori dealt with Katie's death, she came to new life in Jesus.

Lori wonders if the Gentiles to whom Luke writes were similarly touched by the widow's story. She says, "This could speak to the Gentiles who hadn't been raised with the Scriptures and who wouldn't necessarily call out to the God of the Jews. This would be like many of us today, the unsaved, who really don't know *Who* to call out to. But Jesus comes and meets us anyway."

One good-bye became the beginning of a hello in eternity; for Lori knows that one day she will meet Katie again. Though Katie wasn't raised from the dead, in effect, Lori was. Two weeks after Katie's death, Lori began sharing her story. Years later, the Lord blessed Lori and her husband with the surprise of Benjamin, Katie's little brother.

Jesus' Words in Action: Jesus knew the widow's loneliness. He met her needs even though she didn't ask for help. How about you? Do you wonder if Jesus knows your pain? Jesus is coming. Meet Him at the gate, and let Him take care of you. He *does* notice loneliness, death, and sorrow, and He *does* want to respond.

Or do you know someone who needs the Savior's comfort? In prayer today, ask the Lord to place someone on your heart.

> Two separate crowds witness the compassion of Christ as well as His resurrection power.

> If you stood in Jesus' crowd, how would you feel about your teacher? If you were a mourner in the other crowd, what would you be thinking about Him?

> "The LORD is close to the broken-hearted and saves those who are crushed in spirit." (Psalm 34:18)

Be the hands and heart of Jesus and reach out at the gate with words of comfort, love, and hope.

Works Cited

1. Bishop, Jim, *The Day Christ Died: The Inspiring Classic in the Final 24 Hours of Jesus' Life* (San Francisco: Harper, 1957), 51.

2. Richards, Sue and Larry, *Every Woman in the Bible* (Nashville, TN: Thomas Nelson, 1999), 160.

3. Yancey, Philip, *The Jesus I Never Knew* (Grand Rapids, MI: Zondervan, 1995), 153–154.

4. Richards, 153.

5. Bishop, 50.

6. Richards, 158–159.

7. Ibid.

8. Weaver, Joanna, *Having a Mary Heart in a Martha World: Intimacy with God in the Busyness of Life* (Colorado Springs, CO: WaterBrook Press, 2000), 52.

9. Higgs, Liz Curtis, *Mad Mary: A Bad Girl from Magdala, Transformed at His Appearing* (Colorado Springs, CO: WaterBrook Press, 2001), 184.

10. Yancey, 153.

11. Richards, 159.

12. Ibid.

13. De Boer, Esther, *Mary Magdalene: Beyond the Myth* (Harrisburg, PA: Trinity Press International, 1996), 36.

14. Ibid., 32

15. Yancey, 153.

16. De Boer, 36

17. Richards, 155.

18. De Boer, 33.

19. Ibid., 34.

20. Gower, Ralph, *The New Manners and Customs of Bible Times* (Chicago: Moody Press, 1987), 70.

21. De Boer, 33.

22. Richards, 166.

23. Ibid., 160.

24. Deffinbaugh, Bob, Th.M, "The Manifestation of Messiah to the Samaritan Woman (John 4:1–42)," http://www.bible.org.

25. Richards, 160.

26. Deffinbaugh, http://www.bible.org.

27. Ibid.

28. Ibid.

29. Ray Vander Laan and Focus on the Family Video (That the World May Know Series), *Faith Lessons on the Life and Ministry of the Messiah: Living Water* (Grand Rapids, MI: Zondervan, 1996, 1998), Volume 3, Video 2.

30. Deffinbaugh, http://www.bible.org.

31. Ibid.

32. Richards, 180.

WEEK THREE

Traveling with Jesus

Seven Women Who Met Jesus

Monday: A Sinful Woman Anoints Jesus

In the next three weeks we're going to meet the women in the Bible who encountered Jesus. What a privilege to be taught, loved, healed by Him.

📖 Read Luke 7:36–50.

1. How would you describe the woman who anoints Jesus' feet? *She wants repentent of her past immoral life style. She washed Jesus' feet with her tears & dried them with her hair in gratitude for His grace for her.*

Each of the Gospels tells of Jesus being anointed by a woman (Matthew 26:7–13; Mark 14:3–9; Luke 7:36–50; John 12:1–8). Some readers interpret the four passages as being three *different* women with Matthew and Mark covering the same anointing. Some believe that *all* the passages are about the *same* woman. Some believe that *three* of the passages refer to Mary of Bethany, while the other refers to an unnamed sinner. Though there are many similarities in the passages, the differences in the Luke 7 passage lead me to believe that this anointing is different from the anointing Jesus receives near His death. I am inclined to read the four passages as at least two separate accounts: the sinner woman anointing Jesus early in His ministry, and Mary, sister of Martha, anointing Jesus the week before His crucifixion.

But before we look at the passage, let's remove any misconceptions we may have. This Luke passage never names the sinner woman as Mary Magdalene. Much has been attributed to Mary Magdalene that may not belong to her. Tomorrow we will explore what the Bible *does* say about her in depth. Suffice it to say, this woman of Luke 7 loved and anointed Jesus and remains *unnamed* but not *unloved* by the Lord.

2. Who is hosting the event? In what ways is the woman a stark contrast to the host? *One of the Pharisees. This woman no position or worth in a man's world.*

A Pharisee hosting Jesus was revolutionary enough! But now a woman enters his home. The home of a Pharisee? Culturally this just did not happen. Plus, what do we know about her? Not only is she sinful, she's led a sinful life *in that town.*

3. How might those in the house know of her past? *Through talk or perhaps they used her services.*

4. List the actions she takes to honor Jesus (verses 38, 44–46). *– Washed His feet with her tears; dried them with her hair & applied an expensive alabaster perfume.*

Are you surprised about her use of hair? Don't be. In the first century, a master sometimes dried his hands on a servant's hair.[1] After walking in sandals through dusty streets, having one's feet washed and massaged would have been customary and welcomed. At His entry, she honors Him as Lord in a way no one else did.

> The jar has to be broken to release the sweet perfume. In what ways do we need to be broken to release our sweetness?

The perfume she carries is a costly, aromatic liquid made from the root of an Indian plant. The Old Testament refers to this substance in Song of Songs 1:12; 4:13, 14. She carries this perfume in an alabaster jar, a soft substance that looks like marble. Because alabaster boxes of this time often hold perfume, most containers filled with perfume are called alabaster whether they are or not. To release the perfume, the vessel has to be broken.[2]

Though there were rules against touching or talking, Jesus does not recoil at the woman's touch. For Jesus to be anointed by a woman who was known to be sinful is culturally and religiously taboo. No self-respecting Pharisee would have allowed himself to be made ceremonially unclean by a known sinner.

5. How do the Pharisees respond ? (verse 39)? *If this man was a prophet, he would know what kind of woman was touching him. She is a sinner.*

Jesus then responds to the Pharisee's judgmental grumbling by teaching with a parable, a beautiful story about two men owing money and a moneylender who forgives them. The one man's debt is five hundred denarii (500 days' wages) and the other owes fifty denarii (50 days' wages). Thus, one man is forgiven about seventeen months' income, while the other is forgiven about two months' worth.

Jesus draws a parallel: the woman who anointed him is the debtor forgiven five hundred denarii, and the Pharisee is the debtor forgiven one-tenth that amount. Jesus contrasts what she has done for Him with what the Pharisee failed to do. To anoint a king's head with oil is similar to a current-day crowning (1 Samuel 16:13; 2 Samuel 5:3; 1 Kings 1:39). She treated Him like a king, literally.

6. As Jesus relates this story, how do you think this woman feels? In her humbled position, tears streaming down her face, what is going through her mind? *unworthy & grateful.*
She probably wonders at his care for her.

7. Write down what Jesus says to her. *Your sins are forgiven.*

This woman lavishly loves the One who changed her life. We don't hear that she *asks* for forgiveness, but her loving and respectful actions *beg* for it.

8. Describe the change in this woman's feelings and life from the time she enters the home until she leaves. *She was bold enough to touch Jesus' outstretched arm wash his feet. She probably approached him with trepidation but left with a heart filled with joy.*

9. How is she similar, yet different, from the woman at the well? *Jesus initiated the conversation with the woman at the well. She did not deny her sin. She left to shared the Good News that the Messiah was there.*

10. How is Jesus' response to her similar to His response to the adulterous woman? *He equally forgave them. We do not know if this woman was Jewish but certainly the woman at the well was Samaritan. That made no difference in their forgiveness.*

Jesus' Words in Action: Two thoughts: forgiveness feels so good and forgiving, is so freeing!

What about you? Are you in need of forgiveness from God or from your neighbor, friends, or family? If there is a long-outstanding wrong, it's time to ask forgiveness. Or has someone wronged you? Has the debt of fifty denarii driven a spike of anger, bitterness, and resentment into your heart? Is it time to forgive the debt of fifty denarii you feel is owed to you since Jesus has forgiven you of so much more?

Jesus exalts this woman. She is remembered. Because He sets this up as such a positive example, we need to study this story and incorporate her good qualities in our lives.

What can we learn from this woman's act of worship? How can we emulate it today? Jesus exalts her. How can you lavishly honor the Lord with your time, talents, and finances? Do you reveal that you've been loved much and forgiven much? *She gave what she had out of love & gratitude*

Tuesday: The Real Mary Magdalene

One year I was asked to play Mary, Mother of Jesus in our local passion play. But later, the director asked if I could switch and play a different Mary: Mary Magdalene. My preschooler was disappointed. She felt hurt that I was demoted to playing a "crazy lady."

I'm not sure where my daughter came up with that idea, but misconceptions about Mary Magdalene abound. Whole books have been written about her. The Bible first mentions Mary Magdalene in Luke 8:1–3:

> *After this, Jesus traveled about from one town and village to another, proclaiming the good news of the kingdom of God. The Twelve were with him, and also some women who had been cured of evil spirits and diseases:* Mary (called Magdalene) *from whom seven demons had come out; Joanna the wife of Cuza, the manager of Herod's household; Susanna; and many others. These women were helping to support them out of their own means. (Luke 8:1–3)*

1. Twelve male disciples followed Jesus. Who else was there?
Mary Magdalene
Joanna
Susanna

Matthew and Mark record that certain women followed and cared for Jesus' needs (Matthew 27:55–56; Mark 15:40–41). A group of women are hearing the stories of Jesus, believing, and committing their lives and their finances to His work. They may have temporarily or on a day-to-day basis left their families and their homes to follow Him. Some have been forgiven much, so they forgive much.[3] Mary is the leader of these women. But before we say who she *is*, let's talk about who she is *not*.

What's your first reaction to Mary Magdalene?

Specifically, the Bible does *not* say Mary Magdalene is a prostitute. The Bible does *not* say that she is the sinner woman who anoints Jesus. As a matter of fact, Liz Curtis Higgs' fascinating book *Mad Mary: A Bad Girl from Magdala* points out that in Luke 7 the sinner who anoints Jesus is *unnamed*, whereas at the beginning of Luke 8, Mary Magdalene is introduced completely unrelated to the previous passage. Jesus tells the sinner woman of Luke 7 to go in peace, not to come follow Him.[4]

Because artists have long depicted a repentant and worshipful Mary Magdalene, this is the picture we are left with. Another false picture comes from the portrayal in film and literature that Mary Magdalene is the wife of Jesus and mother of His child. Now remove artistic interpretation and previous misconceptions to focus on what the Bible says about the woman who is second only to the Mother of Jesus in New Testament coverage. Hold onto this one fact: Mary follows Jesus to the cross and beyond. She is so changed by His power to transform that she has faith when others walk away.

The Mary confusion is complicated by the many other Marys discussed in the New Testament. This list may help you sort them out as we study:

The *Other* New Testament Marys

- Mary of Nazareth, mother of Jesus
- Mary, the wife of Clopas (John 19:25)
- Mary, mother of James and Joses (Matthew 27:56; Mark 15:40; Luke 24:10)
- Mary of Bethany, sister of Lazarus and Martha (Luke 10:39)

- Mary of Jerusalem, mother of Mark (Acts 12:12)
- Mary of Rome (aide to Paul, Romans 16:6)
- The *other* Mary (Matthew 27:61; 28:1)

While other Marys are defined by their families, Mary Magdalene is defined by her hometown of Magdala.[5] The Greek form of Magdalene is *Migdol* or *watchtower*.[6]

In AD 30 Magdala is a trading village on the Sea of Galilee (see map on p. 14). Not only is it the center of trade in salt fish, material, and agriculture, it also is a juncture of religions and customs represented by the Jewish and Hellenistic faiths.[7] Thus, Magdala feels the oppression, repression, and violence of Roman occupation.[8]

2. Look back at Luke 8:1–3. What do we know about the backgrounds of these female followers? How has Jesus touched their lives? *They are identified by their family relationships. They provided financial support for Jesus & the disciples.*

Liz Curtis Higgs explains,

> He healed them, delivered them, saved them, empowered them. And though it's not recorded in Scripture, he may have called these women to share the gospel publicly as well. It's clear he counted them among his closest disciples. He gave their lives meaning in a culture that did not always value women.[9]

3. If we transferred Mary Magdalene's life to the screen, what scenes would be missing? In other words, what more would you like to know about her? *How did she survive prior to knowing Jesus.*

According to Luke 8, at some point in Mary's life, seven demons entered her. Demonic oppression was very real in New Testament times. In *Mad Mary*, Liz Curtis Higgs speculates that some may doubt the existence of demons. However, she points out the following three facts:

1. Jesus himself acknowledges the existence of demons and evil spirits (Matthew 12:28; Luke 11:24).
2. Jesus speaks to demons (Mark 8:31–32; Mark 9:25).
3. The demons speak back to him (Luke 4:41).[10]

Besides, why would Jesus spend any of His precious time casting out something that doesn't exist? (Matthew 8:28–34; 12:22–32; Mark 3:22–27; 5:1–20; Luke 8:26–39; 11:14–23) The demons often understand who Jesus is and believe in Him. If ever there was a time when Satan should have been fighting, it was when God came to earth.

Mary had not one, but seven demons cast out. Wouldn't it be nice to see a "before and after" picture? Though the disciples may have witnessed Mary Magdalene's deliverance from demon oppression, it's not recorded.

If you need to get an idea what the "before" picture might have looked like, flip to Luke 4:35 to see Jesus cast out a demon. Luke 8:26–39 and Mark 5:1–20 also describe a naked, demon-possessed, previously chained man living in the tombs. The demon-possessed man has broken free of his chains and "been driven by the demon into solitary places" (Luke 8:29). "No one was strong enough to subdue him" (Mark 5:4). Night and day the man cries out and cuts himself with stones. The evil spirit in him has seized him many times. When Jesus arrives, He gives the demons permission to enter two thousand pigs. Then the pigs rush off a steep bank and drown.

> "They found the man from whom the demons had gone out, sitting at Jesus' feet, dressed and in his right mind." (Luke 8:35)

What happens when demons leave a person? There is instant change that all can see.

After Jesus casts out the demon, the change in the man is so dramatic, the people become afraid, and ask Jesus to leave. The healed man begs to go with Jesus, but Jesus has a mission and purpose for this liberated man. " 'Return home and tell how much God has done for you.' So the man went away and told all over town how much Jesus had done for him" (Luke 8:39). His before and after picture is profound.

Based on the unattractive picture of the demon-possessed man, maybe we don't really want to see Mary Magdalene's "before" picture.[11] I can't presume what Mary's life was like prior to meeting Jesus, but if being possessed in body, mind, and personality by *seven* demons is anything like this man's torment and anguish, we know that Mary's life must have been hell on earth. Is it any wonder she freely follows the One who has liberated her? Jesus has a plan and a purpose for her life: follow, learn, and lead.

4. Considering the background information above, list words to describe Mary Magdalene's situation prior to meeting Jesus.

Cast out, a source to be feared, distraught, hopeless.

Mary chooses to follow Jesus. From town to town, she listens to Him, watches Him heal, and helps support His ministry. During this time she is a part of His inner circle of disciples. How do we know this? Let's jump way ahead to resurrection day and Mary Magdalene's encounter with the angel at the empty tomb, which we will study later in Week 7. In *Mary Magdalene: Beyond the Myth*, Esther De Boer points out that the angel reminds the women that they had already heard Jesus tell them He would rise from the dead.[12]

> *In their fright the women bowed down with their faces to the ground, but the men said to them, "Why do you look for the living among the dead? He is not here; he has risen! Remember how he told you, while he was still with you in Galilee: 'The Son of Man must be delivered into the hands of sinful men, be crucified and on the third day be raised again.' " Then they remembered his words.* (Luke 24:5–8)

They *remembered* Jesus' words because they had been there *in person* when He prophesied. When did He say it? De Boer encourages us to go back to Luke 9:18–22, which describes Jesus praying in private with His disciples nearby.

God said to Moses, "I AM WHO I AM. This is what you are to say to the Israelites: 'I AM has sent me to you.' " (Exodus 3:14)

> *Once when Jesus was praying in private and his disciples were with him, he asked them, "Who do the crowds say I am?" They replied, "Some say John the Baptist; others say Elijah; and still others, that one of the prophets of long ago has come back to life." "But what about you?" he asked. "Who do you say I am?"*
> *Peter answered, "The Christ of God." Jesus strictly warned them not to tell this to anyone.*
> *And he said, "The Son of Man must suffer many things and be rejected by the elders, chief priests and teachers of the law, and he must be killed and on the third day be raised to life." (Luke 9:18–22)*

In other words, De Boer concludes, "The women belong among those disciples who were evidently allowed to be with Jesus even when he withdrew into solitude to pray. The women belong among the disciples who hear things and are told things by Jesus which must remain hidden from others."[13]

This author also speculates that Mary follows because "She had grown up in a city in which the Roman occupation, the opposition to it and the suffering which that brought were tangible. That could have made her receptive precisely to the non-violent, the spiritual and the healing element of the kingdom of God as this took shape in Jesus."[14] Perhaps the diversity of culture and faith in Mary's hometown of Magdala made her more receptive to the idea that Jesus came for all.[15]

But Mary doesn't just love Jesus' *healing touch*, and His *teaching*. Mary loves *Jesus*!

Jesus' Words in Action: In many cases, Mary Magdalene is listed first and appears to be a leader among the women. She supported Jesus, supported His ministry, and led other women. Obviously, Jesus transformed her life. The Gospel writers include her background because it's important. So is yours. Your past may give you the background to make you a leader, counselor, or teacher. Your past reveals where you came from before Christ and how He has transformed you.

Wednesday: Jesus Heals
A Story within a Story

Three *unnamed* but not *untouched* women meet Jesus. Matthew, Mark, and Luke all record this story, but we'll focus on Mark's story, enhanced with details from Matthew and Luke. This is a meaty day because it's a story within a story. A sandwich of sorts framed by Jairus and his daughter.

[handwritten margin note: Jairus was the elected leader of the synagogue. Many synagogue leaders had close ties to the Pharisees. His bowing b/f Jesus was an act of respect & worship.]

The crowd has gathered because they have heard that Jesus heals and casts out demons. Place yourself with his listeners begging for healing.

📖 Read Mark 5:21–43 (Matthew 9:18–26; Luke 8:41–56).

1. What is Jairus' career? Why is this significant (Mark 5:22)? *See above* *[handwritten: Jesus words to Jairus to us: "Don't be afraid. Just have faith." Jesus was motivated by compassion for demon possessed man.]*

2. How does Jairus approach Jesus (Mark 5:22)?
With humility, bowing down in worship.

Inserted into Jairus' daughter's story is a woman who is not *twelve years old*, but who has struggled for *twelve years* with bleeding.

3. What has the woman lost because of her poor health (Mark 5:26)? *Everything. She was an outcast. Suffered from the tx. of many doctors had spent everything she had to pay them. Rejected by family & friends.*

Remember all the rules for women during menstruation? This woman is ritually unclean and should not be touched—not before, during, or immediately after her menstrual cycle.[16] Despite the religious and cultural taboo, this woman touches the edge or fringe of Christ's cloak, the tassels (Luke 8:44). It was believed that touching the tassels could produce forgiveness and healing.[17]

Does the woman know of Jesus' other healings? Does she long to touch or be touched? Does she fear the scorn of those around her as she wriggles through the crowd? Does she hide her face lest she be discovered? Does she hesitate before grabbing the tassels?

> Oh that my eyes would not be distracted by the glitter of the world and would instead only long to see my Savior's face!

4. How does the woman approach Jesus at first (Mark 5:27)? *She came up behind him through the crowd & touched his robe.*

5. How does Jesus respond to her touch (Mark 5:30)? *He was aware that power went out of Him. "Who touched me?"*

6. How do the disciples react to Jesus' question (Mark 5:31)? *They think that this was a ridiculous question as the crowd was pressing upon him.*

7. How does the woman now approach Jesus (Mark 5:33)? *She was trembling as she realized what had happened to her. She fell on her knees before Him & admitted what she had done.*

8. Meanwhile, what do you think Jairus, the synagogue ruler is thinking about the delay with the hemorrhaging woman? *He probably thought how dare she touch him & contaminate Him. All the while he was eager for Jesus to get to his daughter to heal her.*

> "A bruised reed he will not break, and a smoldering wick he will not snuff out. In faithfulness he will bring forth justice." (Isaiah 42:3)

9. What does Jesus say to her? "*Daughter* your *faith* has *made* you. *will* *go* in *peace* and be *cured* from your *affliction*" (Mark 5:34).

In *The Jesus I Never Knew*, Philip Yancey makes this observation about Jesus' nurturing response to the unclean woman.

> Jesus was often "moved by compassion," and in New Testament times that very word was used maternally to express what a mother feels for her child in her womb. Jesus went out of his way to embrace the unloved and unworthy, the folks who matter not at all to the rest of society—they embarrass us, we wish they'd go away—to prove that even "nobodies" matter infinitely to God. One unclean woman, too shy and full of shame to approach Jesus face-to-face, grabbed his robe hoping he would not notice. He did notice. She learned, like so many other "nobodies," that you cannot easily escape Jesus' gaze.[18]

Jesus loved the unlovely, the rejected, those who didn't fit in the crowd, and even those who weren't allowed to be there. Jesus calls this unnamed woman *"daughter."* What a gentle and loving term from a fatherly Jesus.

By verse 35, we move back to story #1.

What do you think Jairus is thinking when he hears the news, " 'Your daughter is dead,' he said. 'Don't bother the teacher any more' " (Luke 8:49). Now what do you think Jairus is thinking and feeling? Does Jairus have any knowledge of Jesus' raising the widow woman's only son from the dead in the village of Nain, twenty miles away? Is Jairus reassured by witnessing the healing of the woman? *He is probably experiencing renewed hope & a feeling of urgency to get to his daughter before it is too late.*

10. What does Jesus say to Jairus? *Don't be afraid. Just have faith.*

Matthew 9:23 reveals the customary weeping and wailing of a funeral: *"When Jesus entered the synagogue leader's house and saw the noisy crowd and people playing pipes, he said, 'Go away. The girl is not dead but asleep.' But they laughed at him. After the crowd had been put outside, he went in and took the girl by the hand, and she got up."*

11. The guests are not allowed to remain. Why do you think Jesus allows only the father and mother and Peter, James, and John, brother of James, to witness the scene? *He did not want followers due to His miracles. He wanted them to believe + follow out of love + faith.*

Let's bring up the lights on the two unnamed females in the room: Jairus' daughter and wife. Although we have no description of the girls' mother, I have an inkling about what she's feeling. When a child of mine has a high fever, I want to be close by. As long as I was near, I thought nothing could harm them.

And so it doesn't surprise me that it's the dad who goes out to find Jesus. But what is Mom thinking while she helplessly watches her daughter slip away? What is she thinking when the mourners come to grieve at her daughter's death? What is she thinking when she sees Jesus take her little girl's hand and say, *"Talitha koum!* (which means, 'Little girl, I say to you, get up!')"* (Mark 5:41).

Mark translates for his Gentile readers and says *immediately* the girl rose and began to walk, astonishing her mother and father.

12. Why do you think Jesus tells the parents not to tell anyone about this? *He did not want ppl. to follow Him because of His miracles.*

13. What might the *mother* or *daughter* be feeling? *The mother is probably overwhelmed with gratitude & possibly became a strong believer*

Jesus' Words in Action: Who are we like in this story? When we have a problem, do we phone or text friends or do we run to Jesus like Jairus? In what ways do we need to be more like the hemorrhaging woman and reach for Jesus with courage and faith?

Our lives may seem as though they've been hemorrhaging and that nothing can make us whole again. Things have gone wrong for so long, and so many have treated our sickness in so many different ways that we long to just grab onto Jesus. He loves the unlovely, the rejected, those who not only don't fit in the crowd, but those who aren't even allowed to be there. Can we come to Him in faith knowing that we are not unnamed and we are not unloved?

Thursday: The Canaanite's Persistent Faith in Adversity

You've heard about the woman who reached out in faith and was healed. But have you ever reached out in faith and wondered if He heard? Should you keep praying? Let's look at Jesus' teaching.

Not every woman who encountered Jesus had as gentle a reception as the woman who reached for his fringe. I'd almost rather leave this next story out of our study. Jesus doesn't come across quite as compassionate, gentle, and easily moved to heal. In fact, this incident makes me question His approachability. But difficult Bible passages often prompt the most questions and intrigue. Besides, two Gospel writers record the story. Obviously, the words from the Word are here to teach. Now it's up to us to glean Truth.

The woman in this story is a Canaanite. At different times in history, Canaanites worshipped the sun god Baal, and idolatry was often prevalent in this region.

As a Gentile, this woman is not considered by the Jews to be worthy of anything. Yet Jesus is about to reveal some new rules.

An unnamed but not unknown woman comes to Jesus. Her little girl has an unclean spirit, a demon residing in her body. Jesus has been healing diseases, demoniacs, epileptics, and paralytics. Is there any reason he wouldn't heal the mother's daughter?

> "In fact, as soon as she heard about him, a woman whose little daughter was possessed by an evil spirit came and fell at his feet." (Mark 7:25)

📖 Read Matthew 15:21–28 (also Mark 7:24–30). *Jesus is not rejecting the Gentile woman. He may have wanted to test her faith, or he may have wanted to use the situation as another opportunity to teach that faith is available to all people.*

26-28 Dog was a term the Jews commonly applied to Gentiles b/c the Jews considered these people no more likely than dogs to receive God's blessing.

1. Write this woman's plea (Matthew 15:22).

Have mercy on me, O Lord, Son of David! For my daughter is possessed by a demon that torments her severely.

When my first grader was afraid there might be somebody hiding in the attic, each night we would talk to her about how nobody could have slipped in and that Daddy and Mommy could keep her safe. This poor Gentile mother is experiencing something far worse. An evil spirit torments her little girl. What anguish that would bring!

2. What was Jesus' first response to the woman's heartfelt plea (Matthew 15:23)? *At first He gave her no reply.*

What do we do when Jesus is silent? Sometimes we give up. Perhaps someone would have slinked back through the crowd, embarrassed and saddened. But a mother will do anything for a troubled child—even spending her own life's savings on rehabilitation. Now with so many troubling issues: anorexia, bulimia, premarital sex, drug abuse, alcohol abuse, cutting, sexual abuse, we cry out for help and someone to offer hope.

3. But how do the disciples respond to the woman (Matthew 15:23). *They urged Him to send her away b/c she was bothering them with her begging.*

4. Jesus' next response in verse 24 seems strange. "I was sent only to the lost sheep of the house of Israel." What does He mean? *His message was to be to the Jews first. They were to be God's messengers to the world.*

In John 10:16, Jesus reveals that He has come to bring in the *other* sheep. "I have other sheep that are not of this sheep pen. I must bring them also. They too will listen to my voice, and there shall be one flock and one shepherd" (John 10:16).

The woman's faith is great, and she listens to the voice of the Shepherd. Like most mothers, this Canaanite would not give up hope that her daughter would heal. She persists in the face of adversity. She cries out with the title, "Son of David"!

5. In Matthew 15:25, what is her next step? *She worshiped Him, then continued pleading.*

As if His silence and then restrictions were not enough, Jesus adds, "It is not good to take the children's bread and throw it to the dogs" (Matthew 15:26). *Dogs - a term for Gentiles.*

Why would Jesus call this woman and her daughter *"dogs"*? Will the mother stick around for more? Bible commentator Matthew Henry writes that this story teaches that there...

> "A bruised reed he will not break, and a smoldering wick he will not snuff out, till he leads justice to victory. In his name the nations will put their hope." (Matthew 12:20–21)

> may be love in Christ's heart while there are frowns in his face; and it encourages us, though he seems ready to slay us, yet to trust in him. Those whom Christ intends most to honour, he humbles to feel their own unworthiness. A proud, unhumbled heart would not have borne this; but she turned it into an argument to support her request.[19]

Let's look a bit at the translation. According to Ryrie, the children in the illustration are the lost sheep of Israel, and they must be fed before the dogs (Gentiles).[20]

Like the woman who grabs out in faith for the tassel on Jesus' robe, this mother reaches out again and again in words and argument.

6. What does she call Jesus this time? And whose table is she referring to (verse 27)? *Lord — Communion Table?*

7. In keeping with Jesus' analogy, what is she saying that Jesus should do for her daughter (verse 27)? *Feed her*

8. Why does Jesus now respond differently (verse 28)? *She had faith regardless of what appeared to be rejection & the daughter was healed instantly. Jesus said that her faith was great. He granted her request.*

9. What does Jesus proclaim about the woman and also her daughter? (Matthew 15:28)?

Your faith is great! The dau. was healed.

Mark 7:29 adds further information when Jesus says, "For such a reply, you may go; the demon has left your daughter."

The woman doesn't linger in doubt to continue the debate. She must be convinced and reassured. Though she doesn't see the immediate answer to her plea, she shows great faith. Does she *run* all the way home? Mark 7:30 reports that she returns home to find her daughter in bed, and the demon is gone.

I want to see the missing scene. To watch the blessed reconciliation and healing of their relationship. I want to see the mother and daughter in sweet conversation and communion. How does the mother explain the healing to her daughter? "I was so worried about you! Do you know what just happened? What was it like?"

Jesus' Words in Action: Is there something you've longed and prayed for? Have you felt like a dog that the master has not fed? Consider Jesus' story from Luke 18:3–5 about the widow seeking justice. The woman's persistent knocking finally convinces the judge. And if that persistence is so attractive, why do we give up so easily? Fall at His feet and plead your case before the Master. God wants to answer the prayers of His children and He will give you more than scraps!

Friday: Mary and Martha, Act I
(A Short Play in Three Acts)

For the next three days we'll read about two familiar women in an unfamiliar way. We'll study Mary and Martha as a play in three acts.

Consider these two unmarried sisters considering their culture and time. They should have been married by the age of 13. Their father

---

Words of Jesus:

"Ask and it will be given to you; seek and you will find; knock and the door will be opened to you. For everyone who asks receives; he who seeks finds; and to him who knocks, the door will be opened." (Matthew 7:7–8)

has probably died and passed the house on to his only son, Lazarus. Or Martha could have been a widow living in the home of her deceased husband. All that we know is that they are single, and in AD 30, their single status is looked down upon by many.[21]

Mary and Martha

As you learn about Mary and Martha, fill in this Venn diagram.

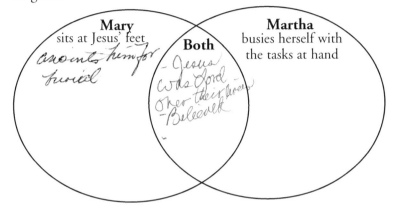

Mary
sits at Jesus' feet
anoints him for burial

Both
- *Jesus was Lord*
- *Over their house*
- *Believed*

Martha
busies herself with the tasks at hand

ACT I:

Location: Bethany
Time: Months prior to death
Cast: *Jesus, Martha, Mary*
Title: *One thing worth being concerned about*

1. Read Luke 10:38–42, then fill in the cast list and title for Act I.

2. What do you know about Martha from verse 38?
Martha welcomed them into their home.

3. What troubles Martha most about the situation (verse 40)? *Mary is not helping with preparations for their guest.*

The woman's role is to serve in the kitchen, not to hang around with the guys, and most certainly not to be taught. But here we have Jesus breaking all the cultural rules by allowing a woman to sit at His feet and absorb His teaching. The *Torah* is for the sons and not for the daughters. One Rabbi of this time goes so far as to say that the words of the Torah should be burned rather than taught to women. But here we have Jesus breaking all the cultural rules by allowing a woman to sit at His feet and absorb His teaching.[22]

4. Write Jesus' response below, but instead of "*Martha, Martha,*" write in your *own* name.

> *Sandy, you are worried & upset over all these details. There is only one thing worth being concerned about. Mary has discovered it & it will not be taken from her.*

5. What could you learn from the words of the Lord?

> *He is to be my primary focus.*

6. In what areas are you:

distracted - *health*
worried - *finances*
bothered - *isolation*

When are you more focused on your church work than on the Lord?

When do you look at what others are doing instead of looking at your own heart?

Do you know someone who is a Mary?

7. If Jesus came to your house today, what would concern you most?

- ■ the outward cleanliness of your home
- ■ the way you look
- ■ what you say to other family members
- ■ the state of your heart
- ■ whether you have a peaceful, loving home

To keep focused, I begin the day with a to-do list scribbled on paper to remind myself of all the things I need to get done. I love to scratch them off one by one. But sometimes I leave off what is most important:

- ■ time in prayer with Jesus
- ■ time in the Word
- ■ loving little moments with my children
- ■ love my husband in tangible ways

I seem to list what makes a visible difference. My heart preparations, time spent with the Lord *do* impact the rest of my to-do list and make a visible difference.

Jesus' Words in Action: What does your list look like for today? How can you put Jesus' words in action? How can you get ready to spend time with Him? What is the *one thing* you need to choose (Luke 10:42)?

[handwritten: ✳ - Time with Him & study / - Love my husband in / tangible ways]

Works Cited

1. Higgs, Liz Curtis, *Mad Mary: A Bad Girl from Magdala, Transformed at His Appearing* (Colorado Springs, CO: WaterBrook Press, 2001), 143.

2. *Easton's Bible Dictionary* in Accordance Bible software. CD-ROM, version 5.7. Oak Tree Software, Inc.

3. De Boer, Esther, *Mary Magdalene: Beyond the Myth* (Harrisburg, PA: Trinity Press International, 1996), 31.

4. Higgs, 144.

5. De Boer, 55.

6. Higgs, 150.

7. Deen, Edith, *All of the Women of the Bible* (New York: Harper and Brothers, 1955), 202.

8. De Boer, 29–30.

9. Higgs, 182.

10. Ibid.,161.

11. Ibid.,170.

12. De Boer, 37.

13. Ibid.

14. Ibid., 41.

15. Ibid.

16. Richards, Sue and Larry, *Every Woman in the Bible* (Nashville, TN: Thomas Nelson, 1999), 109.

17. Ray Vander Laan and Focus on the Family Video Series, "*That the World May Know: Faith Lessons on the Life and Ministry of the Messiah: The Rabbi*" (Grand Rapids, MI: Zondervan, 1996, 1998), Volume 3, Video 2.

18. Yancey, Philip, *The Jesus I Never Knew* (Grand Rapids, MI: Zondervan, 1995), 159.

19. *Matthew Henry Commentary,* in Accordance Bible software. CD-ROM, version 5.7. Oak Tree Software, Inc.

20. *The Ryrie Study Bible,* (Chicago, Illinois: Moody Press, 1976, 1978), 1472.

21. Richards, 158.

22. Ibid.

Following Jesus

Two More Women Touched By Him

God's timing, especially His delays, may make us think he is not answering or is not answering the way we want. But he will meet our needs according to his perfect schedule + purpose.

Monday: Mary and Martha, Act II

Let's move on to Act II of the Mary and Martha drama.

ACT II

Location: Tomb

Time: Months Prior to Jesus' Death *Thos.*

Cast: *Lazarus, Mary Martha, Jesus, Disciples*

Title: *Anyone who believes in me will live.*

1. Read John 11:1–46 and then fill in the cast list and title for Act II.

Lazarus has been dead for four days. Mary and Martha grieve deeply. They both know Jesus is coming, but only Martha runs out to meet Him.

2. What is the purpose of Lazarus' illness and resurrection (John 11:4, 41–42, 45)? And how does this help explain why Jesus lingers an additional two days?

Any trial a believer faces can ultimately bring glory to God b/c God can bring good out of bad situations. Jesus had confidence that God heard him. Many came to believe.

3. Why do you think John inserts verse 11:5?

We are to patiently work on await God's timing.

The disciples recognize that returning to Judea is dangerous and that it may even result in stoning. Jesus knows that it doesn't matter what danger exists; if He's walking in the light of His Father, He will not stumble. Mary and Martha react differently to the news that Jesus is finally arriving (verses 20–21, 30, 32–33).

4. What do both Mary and Martha call Jesus (verses 21, 32)? Return to your Venn diagram on page 51 and note the differences and similarities. *Lord*

5. Martha makes a strong claim in verse 21. If her Lord had been there, what would *not* have happened? In verse 22, she goes even further, What is she asking for? *"If you had been here my brother would't have died. She is asking that Lazarus be restored to life.*

Though Martha understands her brother is a believer and will one day rise again, Jesus uses the opportunity to compare Lazarus with Himself and claims, "I am the Resurrection and the Life" (verses 25–26). We may have previously questioned some of Martha's attitudes and reactions, but just look at how she responds in verse 27.

6. Write her claim in verse 27 below.
"I believe.... *you are the Messiah, the Son of God, the one who has come into the world from God."*

7. What is Jesus' reaction in verses 33 and 35? *He was angered & deeply troubled. Jesus wept. Perhaps he empathized with their grief, or perhaps he was troubled at their unbelief.*

8. What two contrasting opinions do the observers have in verses 36 and 37? *"See how much He loved Him." "This man healed a blind man. Couldn't he have kept Lazarus from dying?"*

Jesus commands the stone to be moved. Though practical Martha knows that Jesus is capable of overcoming any situation, predictably she is concerned about the stench. The crowd then hears Jesus gives thanks for God's answer to a prayer He must have already prayed regarding Lazarus (verse 41).

Again, in verses 45–46, we have two contrasting reactions of the observers and one big *"but"* separating them.

> "Did I not tell you that if you believed, you would see the glory of God?" (verse 40)

It doesn't seem to matter what miraculous acts Jesus does, some still do not believe. Yancey writes, "Although faith may produce miracles, miracles do not necessarily produce faith."[1] Some skeptics watch Lazarus emerge, with his wrappings clinging to His body and a cloth binding His face. Jesus commands the observers to release him from His bonds. But some who witness this resurrection are in greater bondage than Lazarus.

P.S. Our scene should end here, but we need a **P.S.** Something occurs in another location, behind the backs of Lazarus, Mary, and Martha, but certainly not unknown to Jesus.

Jesus' miracles place Him in the center of the radar screen. The chief priests and Pharisees are threatened. The orders are given: if anyone knows where Jesus is, they should report it so He can be arrested. With a death threat hanging over His head, Jesus' mobility is reduced (verses 53–54). This chilling postscript leads us straight into tomorrow's Act III and a partial resolution of our drama.

Jesus' Words in Action: But before *tomorrow*, what have you learned *today*? In both Christ's living and in His dying, Jesus brings life. Martha knew who Jesus was. Jesus claims that He is the resurrection and the life and that believers will never die. He concludes with, "Do you believe this?" That's an important question. If He asked you that today, how would you answer?

Tuesday: Mary and Martha, Act III
Mary Anoints Jesus

Time: Six days prior to Passover
Setting: Bethany
Scripture: John 12:1–11 (Matthew 26:6–16; Mark 14:1–11)
Cast: *Jesus, Lazarus, Martha, Mary, Judas*
Title: Mary Anoints Jesus

The curtain comes down on Act II with Jesus being stalked by His enemies. Now we read the rest of the story. The setting is Bethany, a small, quiet village near the Mount of Olives (see map on p. 16). This strategic location just two miles outside of Jerusalem will become an important home base for Jesus during His final week on earth. Act III occurs six days before

Passover. We're jumping way ahead to just before Jesus rides into Jerusalem on a donkey.

1. What is the role of each of the characters, Mary, Martha, and Lazarus? Record differences in your Venn diagram (p.51).

The Jews decided to kill Lazarus, too, for it was b/c of him that 8 them deserted the Pharisees + believed in Jesus.

2. What actions does Mary take (John 12:3)?

In AD 2000, a person takes off his hat to show respect when entering a home. In AD 30, a person takes off his sandals and washes his feet before entering.[2] And yet, not even a servant is *required* to wash another man's feet.[3] The pure nard was a costly perfume or anointing oil made from an East Indian plant. What Mary pours on Jesus' feet is worth about three hundred denarii, the equivalent of what a commoner could earn in a year. The fragrance fills the room. Mary wipes her hair across Jesus' feet.

3. Read John 12:1–11 and then fill in today's header.

The pure nard was a costly perfume or anointing oil made from an East Indian plant. What Mary pours on Jesus' feet is worth about three hundred denarii, the equivalent of what a commoner could earn in a year. The fragrance fills the room. Mary wipes her hair across Jesus' feet.

> By that act, she laid down her glory and, in essence, stood naked before her Lord. For in that culture, no proper woman ever let her hair down in public. A woman's hair was her glory, her identity, her ultimate sign of femininity, an intimate gift meant only for her husband. But for Mary, nothing was too extravagant for Jesus; she was even willing to risk her reputation. Like a lover before her beloved, she made herself vulnerable and fragile, open for rejection or rebuke.[4]

4. Who is disgusted, and why is he angered (verses 5–6)?

Judas. He said that the nard could have been sold to help the poor. John doubted his motivation.

5. John is privy to a little background information on Judas, which foreshadows Judas' greed. What does John reveal about Judas in John 12:6? *Judas was a thief + helped himself to the treasury.*

6. In your *own words*, write what Jesus says about Mary's generous actions (verses 7–8).

Leave her alone. She is preparing Me for My funeral.

The needs and pleas for help are unending. Some generous women get "battle fatigue" and feel so overwhelmed they can't face any more needs on the frontline. But time spent in lavishly anointing Jesus with love, praise, and thanks will never exhaust us. We need to take time to bless Him; this helps us to continue blessing *others*.

Mary has the opportunity to anoint Jesus while He is still alive. Her action foreshadows Jesus' burial. This scene, and thus the entire play, ends with the ominous prophecy that Jesus will not always be among them on earth, preparing us for Jesus' last week. As we study the Passion Week, remember that this anointing chronologically belongs in that week. Her action demonstrates sacrificial love and worship.

Jesus' Words in Action: Could you write a statement below claiming who you believe Jesus to be? Be a *Martha* and try it. Could you sit at Jesus' feet and spend time with Him? Could you pour out your talents and your wealth in *worthship* or worship of Jesus? Be a *Mary* and try it.

Martha – Jesus is the overcomer – full of power & grace. Mary – Jesus is my Master, my savior, the captain of my soul.

Wednesday: The Bent Woman

Today we'll study an unnamed woman doubled over in sickness. Looking Jesus in the eye must be hard for some of the women Jesus encounters around AD 30. Maybe they are full of shame or unworthiness. The unnamed woman we'll walk beside today is badly stooped with illness. They meet while Jesus is teaching in the synagogue on the Sabbath. Doctor Luke is the only Gospel writer to record this event.

📖 Read Luke 13:10–17.

1. How long had the woman been sick (verse 11)?

2. What caused her sickness (verses 11, 16)?

3. What are the symptoms (verse 11)?

4. How does Jesus heal her (verse 12)?

5. What is the woman's two-part response (verse 13)?

6. Do we know if this woman *asked* for healing? Do we know if she had any faith? What drew Jesus to her side (verse 12)?

7. The synagogue officials are furious over Jesus' work on the Sabbath. What's the officials' argument (verse 14)?

8. Jesus thinks fast. I love His response. "Don't you lead a donkey to water?" (verse 15). And then He calls the woman by name. What is the significance of the title he bestows upon her?

Daughter of _____ (verse 16)

11. What are the reactions of the two groups (verse 17)?

Opponents:
Multitude:

Remember, you're a woman in the crowd. If you listened in just a bit longer, you'd hear Jesus ask a question and answer it with two similes, one of which features a woman kneading bread. Isn't that just like Jesus? There are other women in the audience, and everything He says is also for their benefit (verses 18–21).

Jesus' Words in Action: What do you learn about Jesus today? Jesus noticed people in pain and went out of His way to help them. The result of His loving touch was evident to those who traveled beside Him. What encourages you about this woman's encounter with Jesus? How are you encouraged by what you see Jesus

> When God makes our crooked ways straight, do we immediately stand up and give him the glory?

doing in the lives of those around you? In what ways are we bent? How could our straightening become a great witness to others?

Thursday: Salome's Question

The next woman we'll walk with is a close follower of Jesus. From Matthew 27:56, we know that Salome is most likely the mother of the sons of Zebedee. As the wife of a successful fisherman, Salome is wealthy. We know from Mark's account of James' and John's calling, that their father was in a boat with hired servants. Zebedee must have been able to go on working without the help of his "thunderous" sons.

Like most mothers, she wants the best for her children and for them to have good positions. But Salome is a woman who not only *wants* it; she *asks* for it.

Now let's read Matthew 20:20–28 and meet Salome. Jesus is on His way to Jerusalem when He begins to reveal that He will be mocked, scourged, and crucified. At this point Salome comes up to Jesus, bows down, and asks a question.

1. Write down her question (verse 21).

"_____that one of these ____ _____ of _____ may sit at your _____ and the other at your _____ in your_____."

2. Is Salome's request honest? Is there anything wrong with it? Have you ever felt you asked the Lord for a selfish request? What were the circumstances, and what happened?

3. Jesus answers with a question. "Can you drink the cup I am going to drink?" Who is in the audience answering, "We can" (verse 22)?

4. The answer may not be the one the disciples actually want to hear. What does Jesus mean that they will "indeed drink from His cup"? And why *can't* they sit on His right or His left (verse 23)?

How might Salome have reacted? What if she had walked out of the room in embarrassment and encouraged her sons to leave the ministry? What would she have missed? What do we miss when we don't take correction? Can you remember a time when you accepted criticism with humility and benefited from the experience?

Jesus uses her "selfish" question to re-teach one of His most important messages.

5. Put Matthew 20:26–28, the heart of Jesus' message, into your own words.

Although Salome is rebuked and challenged, she stands corrected, and in Mark 15:40, we learn that she is at the cross with Mary Magdalene and Mary mother of James and Joses. In Mark 16:1, Salome returns to the tomb to bring spices to anoint Jesus' body. She grows from correction and doesn't wilt under chastisement. Thus, she becomes one of the first to know that Jesus has risen from the dead.

6. Ironically, as a postscript, where does John recline at Jesus' Last Supper (John 13:23)?

Jesus hinted that John would outlive the other disciples (John 21:21–25). Later, John was exiled to Patmos and was the last writer to complete his Gospel.

And what about James? Acts 12:1–2 reads, "It was about this time that King Herod arrested some who belonged to the church, intending to persecute them. He had James, the brother of John, put to death with the sword." These two brothers were probably the first and last disciples (except for Judas) to die.

Jesus' Words in Action: Jesus called us to serve and gave us the perfect example of service.

Scripture: "Your attitude should be the same as that of Christ Jesus: Who, being in very nature God, did not consider equality with God something to be grasped, but made himself nothing, taking the very nature of a servant, being made in human likeness." (Philippians 2:5–7)

These verses from Philippians would have helped Salome. Jesus made Himself *nothing*. He left the right hand of God in heavenly places, to take on the nature of a servant. Pray for ways you can serve others with the attitude of Christ.

Friday: An Overview of Last Week

Today's reading is for background on the Gospel writers, geography, politics, people, and timeline. Fold over this page for reference when you have questions.

Gospels:

Each Gospel was written for a particular audience and thus with a specific and unique emphasis. Each writer had a different background. Matthew was a Jewish tax collector writing for the Jews. He emphasized Jesus as Messiah and the fulfillment of Old Testament prophecy. Missionary Mark focused almost half of his book on the last week of Jesus' life. Luke is a doctor with an eye for detail. Matthew, Mark, and Luke are known as the *Synoptic Gospels* because of their similarity. They provide a synopsis of His life from start to finish. John's Gospel differs greatly as you will soon find out.

> "You will indeed drink from my cup, but to sit at my right or left is not for me to grant. These places belong to those for whom they have been prepared by my Father." (Matthew 20:23)

Mark is the shortest gospel. John Mark, a fellow missionary friend of Paul and Barnabus, is the author. Whereas Matthew included a genealogy and much prophecy, Mark omitted these for his Gentile readers. But he did interpret certain Aramaic words (Mark 3:17; 5:41; 7:34; 15:22) for Romans, who might not have been familiar with them. He also used Latin on occasion instead of Greek (Mark 4:21; 6:26, 42; 15:15, 16, 39).[5] In the Book of Mark, everything happens quickly and immediately, moving the reader towards Christ's death and resurrection.

The fact that the New Testament begins with the Gospel of Matthew is significant because Matthew's Gospel connects Old Testament prophecy with New Testament fulfillment.[6] With almost 130 Old Testament references, Matthew quotes from the Old Testament more than the other Gospel writers. Because Matthew is writing to the Jews, he emphasizes Jesus as the Messiah they have long awaited. Watch for his frequent phrase, "that what was spoken through the prophet might be fulfilled."[7] Before becoming a disciple, Matthew collected taxes in Capernaum. He is the only one to cover the magi's visit, Mary's, Joseph's, and Jesus' escape to Egypt, and the Sermon on the Mount.[8]

Mark and Matthew are similar, but almost half of Luke's Gospel is unique.[9]

Physician Luke presents Jesus as the Son of Man to his Gentile audience. His presentation reveals a sympathetic, compassionate Savior. Luke is the one most likely to write about women[10] and often pairs men and women in his stories, giving the women the more favorable depiction.[11]

John's Gospel will give you a whole new perspective. John is the brother of James and one of the sons of Zebedee and Salome. John was a wealthy Jew, a fisherman called by Christ a "son of thunder" (Mark 3:17), and he was recognized as the "disciple whom Jesus loved" (John 21:20, 24). John focuses on many of Jesus' final teachings and emphasizes salvation and eternal life. His writings highlight that since the beginning, God and Jesus were One. Jesus was here long before AD or BC, before all time. The book of John records the seven "I am" claims we studied in Week One, but it specifically focuses on only seven of Jesus' miracles.[12]

Digging Deeper. If you want to get an overview of all four Gospel accounts of the last week of Jesus' life, here are the passages you need.

Text	Audience	Occupation	Emphasis
Matthew	Jews	Tax collector	Jesus is Messiah
Mark	Romans and Gentiles	Missionary	Jesus as Servant and Savior
Luke	Gentiles	Doctor	Jesus is Son of Man
John	All	Fisherman	Jesus is Son of God

Skim-read Matthew 21—28, Mark 11—16, Luke 19:28—Luke 24, John 12:12—John 21. This is a tremendous exercise. Read it as if you don't know "the rest of the story." Place yourself in the audience. What is new or unfamiliar?

Jerusalem Overview

WANTED: YESHU HANNOZRI

He shall be stoned because he has practiced sorcery and enticed Israel to apostasy. Anyone who can say anything in his favor, let him come forward and plead on his behalf. Anyone who knows where he is, let him declare it to the Great Sanhedrin in Jerusalem.[13]

During Passover in AD 30, Jerusalem's population has swelled from fifty thousand residents to perhaps a quarter of a million or even two to three million.[14] The crowded city spills over into tents outside the walls. The Jewish pilgrims cannot understand that this would be the most significant Passover in history. This Passover would end all need for future Passovers. Once this Passover lamb is crucified, His blood would cover all sins for every person forever.

Today we'll look at the geography of the city and its people. As you read, underline key words, points, or characters that are unfamiliar, or make notes in the margins so you can return to these pages as reference material for the final weeks of our journey.

Geography: Map of New Testament Jerusalem

Jerusalem, a three-hundred acre city with a circumference of three miles, is centrally situated between the Mediterranean and Dead seas in the dry hill country. This intersection marks a central point for trade routes. At various times, Persians, Greeks, and Romans occupied Jerusalem's walled city. In 37 BC, King Herod had Jewish workers construct strong walls, a fortress, a moat, the Herodium, and aqueducts. The architecture *was* phenomenal; we say *was* because the city of Jerusalem was eventually destroyed in AD 70 just as Jesus had prophesied.

Looking at the map on the next page, you'll see King Herod's Palace and the Kidron Valley (at the foot of the Mount of Olives/Offense where the Garden of Gethsemane exists). Looking at the map, within the city walls you will find Golgotha, and the Praetorium. Jesus did not remain in the city each evening; more likely He stayed in Mary and Martha's home in nearby Bethany or in the Garden of Gethsemane.

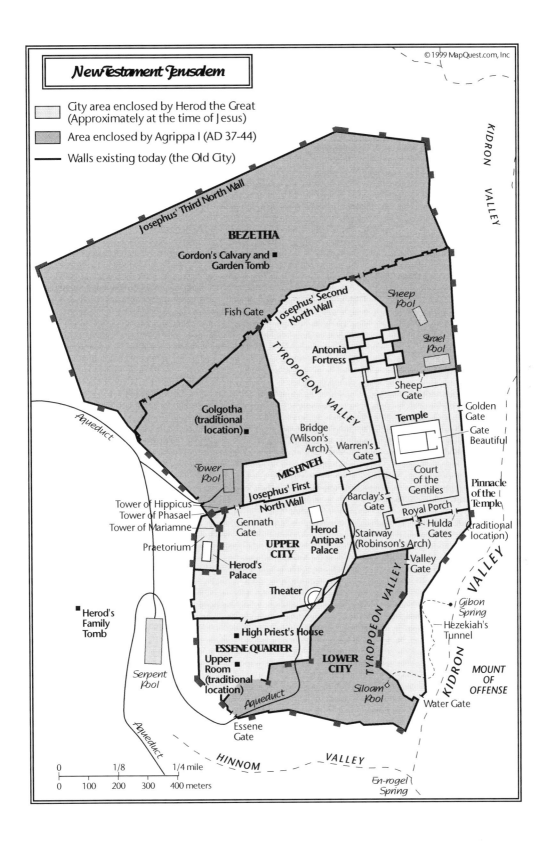

New Testament Jerusalem

© 1999 MapQuest.com, Inc

City area enclosed by Herod the Great
(Approximately at the time of Jesus)

Area enclosed by Agrippa I (AD 37-44)

Walls existing today (the Old City)

KIDRON VALLEY

Josephus' Third North Wall

BEZETHA

Gordon's Calvary and ■
Garden Tomb

Josephus' Second North Wall

Sheep Pool

Fish Gate

Antonia Fortress

Israel Pool

TYROPOEON VALLEY

Sheep Gate

Golden Gate

Temple

Gate Beautiful

Aqueduct

Golgotha (traditional location) ■

Bridge (Wilson's Arch)

Warren's Gate

Court of the Gentiles

Tower Pool

MISHNEH

Josephus' First North Wall

Barclay's Gate

Pinnacle of the Temple

Tower of Hippicus
Tower of Phasael
Tower of Mariamne

Gennath Gate

Herod Antipas' Palace

Royal Porch

Stairway (Robinson's Arch)

Hulda Gates

(traditional location)

Praetorium

UPPER CITY

Valley Gate

KIDRON VALLEY

Herod's Palace

Herod's Family Tomb

Theater

Gihon Spring

Hezekiah's Tunnel

High Priest's House

ESSENE QUARTER

Upper Room (traditional location)

LOWER CITY

TYROPOEON VALLEY

MOUNT OF OFFENSE

Serpent Pool

Aqueduct

Siloam Pool

Water Gate

Aqueduct

Essene Gate

HINNOM VALLEY

| 0 | 1/8 | 1/4 mile |

| 0 | 100 | 200 | 300 | 400 meters |

En-rogel Spring

Major Political and Religious Leaders:

The major political and religious players are all men. Though they may be difficult to relate to, remember: these are real people with names and personalities and hopes and dreams. How do they affect the lives of women in Jerusalem at that time? The one woman on the list (Pilate's wife) is the lone voice of reason.

King Herod the Great was king at Jesus' birth. He was so frightened by the baby that he had all male babies two years and younger in Bethlehem slain. Herod's accomplishments include rebuilding Jerusalem's temple and creating a port city in Caesarea on the Mediterranean Sea.

King Herod had many sons. His sons include Herod Antipas, Archelaus, Herod Philip I, and Herod Phillip II.[15] At King Herod's death in 4 BC, his territories were divided among his descendants. The next generation of Herods was also ruthless. (In Matthew 2:22–23, Joseph and Mary do not return from Egypt to Judea because Archelaus is ruler. They choose instead to settle in Nazareth in Galilee, fulfilling the prophecy that Jesus would be a Nazarene).

Archelaus is the son who ruled Samaria, Judaea, and Idumaea (4 BC–AD 6). Because of his inability to govern, he lost his authority to an appointed prefect or procurator. Procurator Pontius Pilate later assumed Archelaus' region except for the area of Galilee and Perea, which was governed by Archelaus' *brother* Herod Antipas.[16] Can you see why Jesus is later ping-ponged back and forth from Pilate to Herod Antipas? Whose responsibility is Jesus anyway?

Herod Antipas is the son who ruled Galilee and Perea and had John the Baptist beheaded. Jesus called him "that fox" (Luke 13:32). Herod Antipas interrogated Jesus, hoping to see Him perform a miracle or two, and then ridiculed Him (Matthew 14:1–10; Mark 6:14–28; Luke 3:1, 19, 20; 13:31; 23:7–12). He was a political enemy of Pilate until uniting against Jesus. "That day Herod and Pilate became friends— before this they had been enemies" (Luke 23:12).[17] Herod Antipas was later deposed.

Herod Agrippa I is the grandson of Herod the Great and ruled from AD 37–44 over the large region of Palestine, which included Samaria and Judea. He persecuted members of the early Church, imprisoned Peter, and killed James. His death, like his grandfather's, was ugly (Acts 12:21–23).

Annas was the "former" high priest (AD 7–14). His daughter married Caiaphas, who assumed or shared leadership with Annas as president of the Sanhedrin. The Roman procurator deposed him.

Caiaphas served as high priest from AD 27–36 and was Annas' son-in-law and successor to the high priest. Caiaphas, along with the Sanhedrin, voted to have Jesus killed, though Caiaphas tried to pass off responsibility to the Governor of Rome. He is most remembered for his prophetic comment in which he says it would be better "that one man die for the people than that the whole nation perish" (John 11:49–52).

> "Foxes have holes and birds of the air have nests, but the Son of Man has no place to lay his head." (Matthew 8:20)

Pontius Pilate was the sixth Roman procurator and believed in many gods.[18] He served from AD 26–36 as Jerusalem's governor and Rome's representative from afar. The governor usually stayed in Caesarea and preferred Rome for its theatre and excitement. But he came to Jerusalem during times of trouble, an uprising, or when great crowds gathered, such as during Passover. Pilate hated the Jews and had little regard for their religious practices. "Now there were some present at that time who told Jesus about the Galileans whose blood Pilate had mixed with their sacrifices" (Luke 13:1). Because of his ignorance of their religious practices, he made grievous and sometimes idolatrous errors and earned their disrespect, which lessened his authority.

Pilate's wife had more sense (or was scared "senseless" by a dream) and tried to warn him of the danger of convicting an innocent man. Pontius Pilate's famous line is, "What is truth?" Though the *Way* the *Truth* and the *Life* stood before him, he didn't recognize Him. After Pilate falsely slaughtered hundreds of Samaritans near Gerizim, his political career dissolved.[19]

Jews had some legal status and religious freedom, but they were persecuted for their faith. They were set apart because they didn't believe in the Greek and Roman gods; they practiced unusual religious customs, didn't work on the Sabbath, held no political positions, and avoided certain foods.

Beginning in roughly 145 BC, the Jews divided into groups including the Essenes, Pharisees, and Sadducees. These factions believed in various degrees of political separation. Studying their motivations will help you understand their animosity toward Jesus. Some believed in collaboration with Rome while others wanted separation.

Many of the groups listed are clearly collaborationists or separationists. The Pharisees wanted both to be separate and to collaborate. They were principled but practical. They legalistically followed their Jewish rules but because of past persecution, picked which battles to fight.[20] Understanding their fears and desires will help you see why they would have the Son of God killed. The descriptions below begin with those who desired separation the most and end with the staunchest advocates for collaboration.

Political Continuum

Separationists   Collaborationists

Essenes Zealots   Pharisees   Sanhedrin Sadducees

The Essenes were a mystical pacifist sect formed around 100 BC. As separationists they withdrew and lived in desert caves like monks, committing themselves to purity. While awaiting the Messiah, they lived strict lives with ritual baths, a strict diet, no defecating on the Sabbath, sharing their goods, and wearing no jewelry.[21]

Zealots were separationists who rebelled against Roman authority because they believed only God could be king. Unlike the peaceful Essenes, they believed in physically rebelling against authority. They later became lawless, using a sica or Roman dagger to assault their victims and thereby earning the name *Sicarri*.

Pharisees were both separationists and collaborationists. Pharisee literally means, "to separate."[22] For the most part they wanted to be separate from Roman government, but occcasionally they sided with the Sanhedrin in collaboration efforts with Rome. Although they monitored every letter of the law regarding purity and Sabbath practices, they only gave *lip,* not *heart,* service to their beliefs. They were self-righteous, judgmental, and proud. Jesus repeatedly chastised them, "You hypocrites! Isaiah was right when he prophesied about you: 'These people honor me with their lips, but their hearts are far from me. They worship me in vain; their teachings are but rules taught by men'" (Matthew 15:7–9). With 613 commands (365 of which are prohibitions) they had a lot of work keeping up with the rules![23]

The Sanhedrin was a longstanding group of seventy-one members made up of twenty-four chief priests and forty-six elders including scribes, primarily made up of Sadducees.[24] This could be compared to a Jewish supreme court, with the chief justice voting and ruling as high priest. The Sanhedrin members were collaborationists who wanted to keep everyone in line. Rome allowed them a degree of power, and they gave Rome peace in return. They tried to silence the Jews so there would be no insurrection or revolt. The Sanhedrin was fashioned after Moses' Council in Numbers 11:16[25] and formed near the time of the Maccabees.

The **Chief Priests** were Sadducees who represented the Jews, offered animal sacrifices and prayers, and were examples of the ultimate High Priest to come. They took turns ministering in Jerusalem and had great religious responsibility. Because their power was sometimes purchased, their roles became highly political.

Priests numbered approximately seven thousand at the time of Christ. There were also temple guards and rabbis.[26]

Scribes were the lawyers or secretaries of states, and they were usually Pharisees who taught the oral and written laws in public places.[27]

Elders were men of political, religious, and social authority and influence.

The Sadducees were rich and powerful and loved the profit gained from the temple tax.[28] They did not believe in divine intervention or an afterlife and so they lived their life on earth without fear of consequences or with the goal of rewards. Jesus called them "hypocrites" and a "wicked and adulterous generation" (Matthew 16:1–4; 22:23). They were deists and skeptics who aligned themselves with Romans and King Herod. They did not want to lose their status and worldly comforts. In our continuum they were obviously collaborationists who didn't want anything to alter their current situation.[29]

Herodians were political Jews who followed Herod.

Jerusalem, Spring of AD 30 Timeline of Events

Scholars differ on the exact dates of some of these events, but this overview should give you an idea of the *order*. The major difference many scholars have is whether Jesus was crucified on Thursday versus Friday. There are strong reasons presented for either day. Let this thought intrigue *you* to research further.

Jesus' Words in Action: That's a boatload of information, but hopefully resourceful to you for the last half of your journey to the cross.

Sunday	Monday	Tuesday	Wednesday	Thursday	Friday	Saturday
Jesus enters Jerusalem	Jesus curses fig tree / Jesus cleanses the Temple	Jesus questioned by Sanhedrin, Pharisees and Sadducees / Jesus teaches parables and prophesies / *Anointed by Mary (some believe in this date; others believe it to be previous Saturday)*	Judas meets with religious leaders	Disciples prepare for Passover / Jesus washes disciples' feet / Jesus betrayed by Judas / Passover and Lord's Supper / Jesus prays in the garden / Jesus arrested	Trials: Annas and Caiaphas / Trial: Pilate / Trial: Herod / Trial: Pilate / Jesus walks to Golgotha / Jesus hung on the cross / Jesus buried in Joseph's tomb	Soldiers secure the tomb

Works Cited

1. Yancey, Philip, *The Jesus I Never Knew* (Grand Rapids, MI: Zondervan, 1995), 171.

2. Knight, George W., with Rayburn W. Ray, *The Illustrated Everyday Bible Companion: An All-in-One Resource for Everyday Bible Study* (Uhrichsville, OH: Barbour Publishing, Inc., 2005), 124.

3. Weaver, Joanna, *Having a Mary Heart in a Martha World: Finding Intimacy with God in the Busyness of Life* (Colorado Springs, CO: WaterBrook Press, 2000), 82.

4. Ibid., 171.

5. *Nelson's Complete Book of Bible Maps and Charts* (Nashville, TN: Thomas Nelson, 1996), 327.

6. Ibid., 311.

7. Ibid., 313.

8. Ibid.

9. Ibid., 336.

10. Ibid.

11. Richards, Sue and Larry, *Every Woman in the Bible* (Nashville, TN: Thomas Nelson, 1999), 163–168.

12. *Nelson's Complete Book of Bible Maps and Charts*, 347.

13. Maier, Paul L., *In the Fullness of Time: A Historian Looks at Christmas, Easter, and the Early Church* (Grand Rapids, MI: Kregel, 1991), 114.

14. MacArthur, John, *The Murder of Jesus: A Study of How Jesus Died* (Nashville, TN: Thomas Nelson, 2000), 15.

15. *Nelson's Complete Book of Bible Maps and Charts*, 309–310.

16. Gower, Ralph, *The New Manners and Customs of Bible Times* (Chicago: Moody Press, 1987), 278–280.

17. MacArthur, 177.

18. Ibid., 184.

19. Ibid., 174.

20. Yancey, 63.

21. Ibid., 61.

22. *Easton's Bible Dictionary* in Accordance Bible software. CD-ROM, version 5.7. Oak Tree Software, Inc.

23. J. Hampton Keathley, III, Th.M, "The Contention Among the Pharisees," http://www.bible.org.

24. MacArthur, 103. *The MacArthur Study Bible* (Nashville, TN: Thomas Nelson, Word Publishing, 1997), 1488.

25. MacArthur, 103.

26. Bishop, Jim, *The Day Christ Died: The Inspiring Classic on the Last 24 Hours of Jesus' Life* (San Francisco: Harper, 1957), 40.

27. Ibid., 39.

28. *The MacArthur Study Bible* (Nashville, TN: Thomas Nelson, Word Publishing, 1997), 1488.

29. *Easton's Bible Dictionary* in Accordance Bible software. CD-ROM, version 5.7. Oak Tree Software, Inc.

Yancey, 62.

WEEK FIVE

Passion Week

Entering Jerusalem

Pontius Pilot entered Dame day

Monday: Politics and Prophecy

This day looks long because I've included many of the scriptures for your ease in referencing. Hang in there as the drama builds. Jesus and His followers come from Jericho (over 800 feet below sea level) climbing to Jerusalem (2500 feet above sea level).[1] It's a twisting, dusty path ascending over three thousand feet in twenty miles through a barren and rocky landscape filled with steep ledges.[2] This wilderness area was the setting for the parable of the Good Samaritan and Jesus' forty days of temptation. These "Judean badlands" are crowded with pilgrims arriving for Passover.[3]

Passover is a celebration commemorating the Israelites' liberation from Egyptian bondage. From time to time, radical Jewish insurgents would emerge during these celebrations claiming to be the Messiah, which caused outbreaks and the slaughter of many by the Romans. Crowd-control incidents like these necessitated increased numbers of Roman soldiers.[4]

Jesus enters from the east. What is also intriguing is that on the western side of Jerusalem on that same day, Pontius Pilate entered with a military processional. Such a contrast in leaders.

On that Sunday prior to Passover is lamb selection day, the day each family chooses a perfect lamb for the Passover sacrifice. The Jewish pilgrims cannot understand that this would be the most significant Passover in history. This Passover would end all need for future Passovers. God's timing is deliberate. Jesus enters Jerusalem with the chosen Passover lambs because He *is* the Perfect Lamb chosen by God.[5] Once this Passover lamb is crucified, His blood would cover all sins for every person forever.

📖 Read Luke 19:28–40.

During Passover in AD 30, Jerusalem's population has swelled from fifty thousand residents to perhaps a quarter of a million or even two to three million.[6] The crowded city spills over into tents outside the walls.

What about the ~~women~~ who are part of this crowd? What do they see? I wonder if a military victory matters to a group of women who have been delivered by His love and freed from limiting rules and demons? Perhaps it appealed to them when Jesus used nurturing, feminine, and motherly terms to show how deeply He cared for Jerusalem.

> *O Jerusalem, Jerusalem, you who kill the prophets and stone those sent to you, how often I have longed to gather your children together, as a hen gathers her chicks under her wings, but you were not willing! Look, your house is left to you desolate. I tell you, you will not see me again until you say, 'Blessed is he who comes in the name of the Lord.' (Luke 13:34–35)*

This is the moment Jesus foretold. Now the followers shout the very words of Old Testament scripture Jesus had prophesied. It's also in Old Testament prophecy in Psalms 118:25–27 below. Remember "Hosanna!" means "Save us!"

> *O LORD, save us; O LORD, grant us success.*
> *Blessed is he who comes in the name of the LORD.*
> *From the house of the LORD we bless you.*
> *The LORD is God, and he has made his light shine*
> *upon us.*
> *With boughs in hand, join in the festal procession up*
> *to the horns of the altar.*

1. Underline from Zechariah 9:9 in the margin, what prophecy is fulfilled in this passage.

Why an *unbroken* colt? A colt that had never been sat upon was considered more holy (Numbers 19:2; Deuteronomy 21:3; 1 Samuel 6:7)[7] and true to Matthew's recording of prophecy; he points out that this is what the prophets foretold (Matthew 21:3–5).

The people throw their cloaks on the colt as well as the roads—symbolic of the arrival of a military leader. In 2 Kings 9:13, the entry of King Jehu was heralded with cloaks spread

"Rejoice greatly, O Daughter of Zion! Shout, Daughter of Jerusalem! See, your king comes to you, righteous and having salvation, gentle and riding on a donkey, on a colt, the foal of a donkey." (Zechariah 9:9)

beneath him. With Jesus, the crowd acknowledges their hope in a military hero.[8]

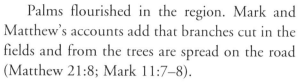

"They hurried and took their cloaks and spread them under him on the bare steps. Then they blew the trumpet and shouted, 'Jehu is king!'" (2 Kings 9:13)

Palms flourished in the region. Mark and Matthew's accounts add that branches cut in the fields and from the trees are spread on the road (Matthew 21:8; Mark 11:7–8).

Even Revelation 7:9 prophesies the use of palms when we greet the Lamb: ". . . from every nation, tribe, people and language, standing before the throne and in front of the Lamb. They were wearing white robes and were holding palm branches in their hands."[9]

Palms were a national symbol for freedom, for zealot freedom fighters, and imprinted on the Jewish coin. Waving a palm branch means, "We will be victorious!" Those hailing Him as King are looking for peace with the wrong battle plan and with politically charged words.[10] This is not the kind of victory the Lamb of God and Prince of Peace had in mind.[11]

They assumed Jesus was a King coming in *might*—a King who would deliver *politically*. However, Jesus came to deliver *spiritually*.

The people knew that a Messiah would come. But His followers gravitated toward a kingly Messiah with power, glory, and authority. This Son of Man would sit at the right hand of God.[12]

Max Lucado writes,

To the Jew the Son of Man was a symbol of triumph. The conqueror. The equalizer. The score-settler. The big brother. The intimidator. The Starship Enterprise. The right arm of the High and Holy. The king who roared down from the heavens in a fiery chariot of vengeance and anger toward those who have oppressed God's holy people.[13]

Jim Bishop adds in *The Day Christ Died*,

In the Psalms, the Messiah is seen in prophecy coming as a king, crushing Israel's enemies, purging Jerusalem, routing nations. After that the Messiah was to govern Palestine in peace and justice, and the

Gentiles would come from the ends of the earth to contemplate the glory of Jerusalem.[14]

What about the women? Do they long for that same sort of King? What do they want to be free from? Let's look back at the Old Testament and see what kind of king the men and women of AD 30 are looking and hoping for.

2. Underline words that people longing for a redeemer may have clung to, hoped for, and focused on.

> For to us a child is born, to us a son is given, and the government will be on his shoulders. And he will be called Wonderful Counselor, Mighty God, Everlasting Father, Prince of Peace. Of the increase of his government and peace there will be no end. He will reign on David's throne and over his kingdom, establishing and upholding it with justice and righteousness from that time on and forever. The zeal of the LORD Almighty will accomplish this. (Isaiah 9:6–7)

"In the future you will see the Son of Man sitting at the right hand of the Mighty One and coming on the clouds of heaven." (Matthew 26:64)

3. Jesus is from Nazareth. The word "Nazareth" may come from the word *netzer* or branch. Continue to select and underline favorite words.

> A shoot will come up from the stump of Jesse; from his roots a Branch will bear fruit. The Spirit LORD of the LORD will rest on him—the Spirit of wisdom and of understanding, the Spirit of counsel and of power, the Spirit of knowledge and of the fear of the LORD—and he will delight in the fear of the LORD. He will not judge by what he sees with his eyes, or decide by what he hears with his ears; but with righteousness he will judge the needy, with justice he will give decisions for the poor of the earth. He will strike the earth with the rod of his mouth; with the breath of his lips he will slay the wicked. Righteousness will be his belt and faithfulness the sash around his waist. The wolf will live with the lamb, the leopard will lie down with the goat, the calf and the lion and the yearling together; and a little child will lead them.

Though Jesus was raised in Nazareth, He was born in Bethlehem. Out of that small village would come a ruler from ancient times. Continue to underline as before.

He will stand and shepherd his flock in the strength of the LORD, in the majesty of the name of the LORD his God. And they will live securely, for then his greatness will reach to the ends of the earth. And he will be their peace. (Micah 5:4–5)

4. The following two prophecies speak of the light for all. As you read and underline these passages, think back to how Jesus healed and liberated those held captive by sickness, demons, or sin.

I, the LORD, have called you in righteousness; I will take hold of your hand. I will keep you and will make you to be a covenant for the people and a light for the Gentiles, to open eyes that are blind, to free captives from prison and to release from the dungeon those who sit in darkness. (Isaiah 42:6–7)

Nevertheless, there will be no more gloom for those who were in distress. In the past he humbled the land of Zebulun and the land of Naphtali, but in the future he will honor Galilee of the Gentiles, by the way of the sea, along the Jordan—The people walking in darkness have seen a great light; on those living in the land of the shadow of death a light has dawned. (Isaiah 9:1–2)

5. Continue underlining words of hope about the Son of Man.

In my vision at night I looked, and there before me was one like a son of man, coming with the clouds of heaven. He approached the Ancient of Days and was led into his presence. He was given authority, glory and sovereign power; all peoples, nations and men of every language worshiped him. His dominion is an everlasting dominion that will not pass away, and his kingdom is one that will never be destroyed. (Daniel 7:13–14)

The Old Testament points to our need for a Savior. God's chosen people longed for peace, safety, freedom, and justice. They wanted a King who would save them from persecution. How could they fathom that it was Jesus' own blood that would bring salvation?

Although the words say Hosanna! Blessed is the King of Israel! Blessed is he who comes in the name of the Lord!"

Their underlying meaning is *"SAVE US! SAVE US! We're sick of Rome! Deliver us! Give us freedom! SAVE US! SAVE US!"*[15]

Save us! Save us! That's just what Jesus longs to do, but from the inside out.

If I were director of a film about Christ, my background music for the Passion Week would have an unending drumbeat. The major key would quickly change to a minor and include great harmonic dissonance to underscore a horrible anticipation.

6. The mood changes. Who ends this joyful scene and why (Luke 19:39)? *Some of the Pharisees in the crowd.*

Now read Luke 19:41–44.

7. We saw Jesus cry at Lazarus' death. What makes him cry in Luke 19? *He wept for Jerusalem b/c they did't accept the opportunity for salvation.*

8. Go back to what you've just underlined from the Old Testament readings. What three words are your favorite descriptors of Jesus. *Wonderful counselor, mighty God, Prince of Peace*

> "From the lips of children and infants you have ordained praise because of your enemies, to silence the foe and the avenger." (Psalm 8:2)

Jesus' Words in Action: The most triumphant scene turns to tears. What would you have thought standing there amongst the crowd? When have you lived through a mountaintop experience only to find yourself in the valley of despair a short time later?

And what about Jesus' longing to nurture? Do you let Him draw you like a mother hen gathers her chicks? Today, carry that picture with you. Let Him tuck you beneath His wings. "Keep me as the apple of your eye; hide me in the shadow of your wings" (Psalms 17:8). And what about the praise? Silence the foe and the avenger by lifting praise to the Lamb of God. Praise is ordained by God!

Tuesday: Turning the Tables:
The Cleansing of the Temple

To fully understand Jesus' wrath in the temple, we need to understand the temple system.

First, Roman coins with Caesar's image cannot be donated for temple tax; they have to be exchanged for Jewish coins. This allows for graft as moneychangers charged exorbitant rates to exchange coins.

Second, the unblemished animal brought for the sacrifice might not pass inspection. To be safe, Jews purchase a marked up lamb that has a greater chance of being declared fit for the sacrifice. These pre-certified sacrifices are high priced. Annas and Caiaphas are the beneficiaries in this moneymaking scheme and they do not want Jesus to ruin their business as usual.[16]

Third, the area filled with pens for sheep, cattle, goats, dove area, pots for sale, oil, salt, and wine booths, and booths for the money exchangers, may also be the Gentile area of worship. How could His Father's house be a house of prayer and worship for *all* people? Jesus doesn't like what He sees.[17]

> "For my house will be called a house of prayer for all nations." (Isaiah 56:7b)
>
> "Has this house, which bears my Name, become a den of robbers to you?" (Jeremiah 7:11a)
>
>

 Read Mark 11:15–17 and Luke 19:45–48 below

The temple area had places off-limits to Gentiles and women. The Court of the Gentiles was where the commerce occurred. The Court of the women was where the women were not allowed beyond.

> *Mark 11:15 On reaching Jerusalem, Jesus entered the temple courts and began driving out those who were buying and selling there. He overturned the tables of the money changers and the benches of those selling doves, 16 and would not allow anyone to carry merchandise through the temple courts. 17 And as he taught them, he said, "Is it not written: 'My house will be called a house of prayer for all nations'? But you have made it 'a den of robbers.'"*
>
> *Luke 19:45 When Jesus entered the temple courts, he began to drive out those who were selling. 46 "It is written," he said to them, "'My house will be a house of prayer'; but you have made it 'a den of robbers.'" 47 Every day he was*

teaching at the temple. But the chief priests, the teachers of the law and the leaders among the people were trying to kill him. 48 Yet they could not find any way to do it, because all the people hung on his words.

1. In contrast to Jesus' entry, what is different about this event? *Jesus was enraged that everyone did have equal access to the temple. Worshippers were taken advantage.*

2. How might those who wanted a military leader been pleased with this reaction? *They might have seen this as a warrior's attack against Rome.*

3. What might you have thought as a woman? Jesus honors His Father but He also cares for the underdog who is being cheated. *It would be hard to accept that Jesus valued women so much.*

4. Where is Jesus quoting from and whose house does He say it is? *Jeremiah 7:11A; God's name.*

5. Considering both passages, what is the reaction of the people to His words? *The people hung on his words but the Pharisees planned to kill Him.*

Jesus' Words in Action: Jesus honored His Father's house and called it a "house of prayer for all nations." How can we honor our Father's house? *By making available to all people.*

Wednesday: Testing and Trickery Q and A

Jesus spends part of Monday through Thursday teaching in the temple. But His teaching is not without questioning. Unfortunately, the questions involve constant testing and trickery. Sometimes Jesus answers with another question, and sometimes Jesus answers with a parable. The interrogators' questions are intended to trap Jesus. Let's look at the Q and A sessions as if they are legal sparring. As you study each questioning session, look at *who* asked the question, *why* the question was asked, and *how* Jesus responds. Place yourself in the crowd of men and women listening to Jesus.

Scripture:	Questioner:	The Question/Why:	Jesus' Response:
1. Matthew 21:23–27 (Mark 11:27–33) (Luke 20:1–8)	Leading priests + elders	By what authority are you doing these things? Hoped to trick him into speaking blasphemy	Did John's authority to baptize come from heaven, or was it merely human?
2. Matthew 22:15–22 (Mark 12:13–17) (Luke 20:20–26)	Pharisees + supporters of Herod	Is it right to pay taxes to Caesar or not? Hoped to entrap him	Why are you trying to trap me? Give Caesar what belongs to Caesar + give God what belongs to God.
3. Matthew 22:23–33 (Luke 20:27–40)	Sadducees	Teacher, if a man dies w/o children, his bro. should marry the widow + have children to carry on his name. Whose wife will she be in the resurrection?	When the dead answer they will be raised
4. Matthew 22:34–40 (Mark 12:28–34)	Pharisees	what is the most imp. commandment in the law of Moses.	You must love the Lord your God w all your heart, soul + mind.

And finally, Jesus has had enough. He lets loose! I wonder what it would feel like to be a woman in the audience hearing one of the most stinging, finger-pointing, and accusatory passages in the Bible, filled with name-calling. (I count at least 14)! If you're having one of those days when you need to vent, read Matthew 23:1–36.

Jesus' Words in Action: As you stood watching the Q and A ping-pong match, were the questions answered? Do you think the questioners asked from a burning desire to know Jesus? When we ask Jesus a question, do we ask truly ready for an answer and a desire to draw closer to Him?

Thursday: The Widow's Offering

If you knew you had a week to live, what messages would you want to impart? A friend of mine with terminal breast cancer planned to videotape messages to her children. If I had to teach my children a few last lessons, I'd want to caution and encourage them about each stage of life. I wouldn't waste time on anything unimportant. I'd want to leave a legacy of inspiration and faith.

Jesus must have wanted His last words to stick. He wanted to prepare His disciples to continue without His physical presence and His male and female followers to remember the last lessons He taught. What follows is a list of Jesus' final lessons up until the Last Supper, excluding His prophecy, and the questioning by religious leaders already studied. Today, we're going to focus on only on Mark's account of the Widow's gift, but if you want to dig deeper, you can fill in the chart at the end of today's study with any of the other points.

Mark 12:41–44 (Luke 21:1–4)
The Widow's Offering

Jesus was in the area of the temple, called the Court of Women.

41 Jesus sat down opposite the place where the offerings were put and watched the crowd putting their money into the temple treasury. Many rich people threw in large amounts. 42 But a poor widow came and put in two very small copper coins, worth only a few cents.

43 Calling his disciples to him, Jesus said, "Truly I tell you, this poor widow has put more into the treasury than all the others. 44 They all gave out of their wealth; but she, out of her poverty, put in everything—all she had to live on."

1. What does this passage teach you about Jesus' concern for widows?

He knew how empoverished they were as widows. She did not give of her surplus, but rather all that she had to live on.

2. Where did Jesus sit and why do you think He did this?

He sat opposite the 7 boxes in which worshippers could deposit their temple tax + the six boxes of freewill offerings in the Women's Court. She gave willingly. Jesus wants us to give everything to Him.

3. Whom did Jesus call together for this lesson and why?

The disciples — this was to show how he expected them to live.

4. What did it mean to give out of wealth vs. giving out of poverty?

Out of wealth was only surplus + costs the giver little. The widow gave all that she had knowing God would care for Her.

5. What might this have demonstrated about the widow?

She was devoted to God's game from her all.

God protects all of them in their destitation.

6. What do the following scriptures have in common?

Psalm 82:3

Defend the weak and the fatherless;
uphold the cause of the poor and the oppressed.

Psalm 68:5

A father to the fatherless, a defender of widows,
is God in his holy dwelling.

Psalm 146:9

The LORD watches over the foreigner
and sustains the fatherless and the widow,
but he frustrates the ways of the wicked.

Exodus 22:22

"Do not take advantage of the widow or the fatherless.

OPTIONAL: If you want to dig deeper and look at other final messages from Jesus, you can fill in the chart below with any of the other points. To ease your research, enter all the scriptures in an online Bible program and you'll have the stories in front of you quickly.

Scripture:	Title of Event	Quote/Point
Matthew 21:18–19 (Mark 11:12–14)	Fig tree cursed	*We are expected to bear fruit for God.*
Mark 11:15–19 (Luke 19:45–48)	The tables are turned	*Jesus wanted them to mirror the expectations of the Scriptures, not take advantage/victimize widows.*
Mark 11:20–25 (Matthew 21:19–22)	Witness of fig tree	*The kind of prayers that move into us in prayer for the fruitfulness of God's kingdom.*
Matthew 21:28–32	Parable of the two sons	*God tells us what to do. We say we will & do not. The second son agreed to go but did not. Are we responding & to Word*
Mark 12:1–12 (Matthew 21:33–45) (Luke 20:9–19)	Parable of the tenants	*God sent the prophets to proclaim God's will & they were killed. Finally, He sent His Son, Jesus. He was murdered as well. The vineyard is the nation of Israel. Tenant farmers are Israel's religious leaders. The other is Gentiles. By telling this story, Jesus exposed the religious leaders' plot to kill him & warned that their sins would be punished.*

Scripture:	Title of Event	Quote/Point
Matthew 22:1–14	Parable of the wedding banquet	*God wants us to join him at His banquet, which will last for eternity. That's why He sends us invitations again & again*
Mark 12:28–34 (Matthew 22:34–40)	The greatest commandment	*Love God & love others*
Matthew 23:37–39	Lament over Jerusalem	*Jesus had ample opportunity to come to Jesus to receive His grace & protection, but instead they rejected Him*
Mark 12:41–44 (Luke 21:1–4)	The widow's gift	*God does & wants our surplus. We are to consider giving – whether money, time or talents; beyond what is convenient*
Luke 21:5–36 (Mark 13:1–37) (Matthew 24:1–51)	Watch out!	*Jesus did not leave his disciples unprepared for the difficult days ahead. He warned them of false Messiahs, natural disasters. However He assured He would be there to protect them*
Matthew 25:1–12	Parable of the 10 virgins	*Be ready for His return*
Matthew 25:14–30	Parable of the talents	*God gives to us, gifts, resources according to our abilities. We are responsible to use well*
Matthew 25:31–46	Separating sheep and goats	*God will separate obedient followers from pretenders & unbelievers*
John 12:20–50	Prophecy fulfilled	*This is a beautiful picture of the necessary sacrifice of Jesus. Jesus died to pay the penalty for our sins*
Matthew 26:1–5 (Mark 14:1–2) (Luke 22:1–2)	Crucifixion Prophecy	*Jesus is prophesying that He will be turned over to be crucified in 2 days fulfilling the scriptures.*
John 12:1–8 (Matthew 26:6–13) (Mark 14:3–9)	Jesus is anointed (Saturday or Tuesday)	*Anticipated Jesus' burial & public declaration of faith in him as Messiah*

Jesus' Words in Action: Once again Jesus notices and cares about a widow. Is it no wonder that Jesus' brother will later write in James 1:27, *"Religion that God our Father accepts as pure and faultless is this: to look after orphans and widows in their distress and to keep oneself from being polluted by the world."*

In light of these words, how does this both reassure and challenge you? *Assurance that God is in charge.*

Friday: What Do the Disciples Know?

As we study the final week of Jesus' earthly life, let's consider what Jesus' listeners know. We know from our study of

Mary Magdalene that she belongs to an inner circle of followers who hear prophecy and hear what people pray. Do they understand how dangerously close they are to separation from their beloved teacher and friend?

Let's look at a few prophetic passages as well as *three* separate warnings Jesus gives to His disciples. In a speech most likely delivered after Jesus cleansed the temple on Monday of Passion Week, Jesus prophesies His death.

> "The stone the builders rejected has become the capstone; the LORD has done this, and it is marvelous in our eyes." (Psalm 118:22–23)

📖 Read John 12:23–36.

1. Who is the kernel of wheat, and how does it produce more seeds (verse 24)? *Jesus. Through His saving grace we are dead to sin. We are to bring others to Jesus — new kernels by sharing the Gd News.*

2. Jesus says in John 12:32, "When I am lifted up from the earth, [I] will draw all men to myself." What does he mean by being *lifted up*? *Because He died.*

Besides this parable and teaching, Jesus prophesies at least three separate times about His death and resurrection. The synoptic Gospels record these prophecies. As you read the passages listed below, note the facts Jesus gives about His arrest, crucifixion, and resurrection.

First Statement: Read Mark 8:30—9:1 (Matthew 16:20–28; Luke 9:21–27).

3. What do the disciples learn about His death from His *first* prophecy? *Will suffer a terrible death, be rejected by the elders, priests & teachers of the law. In 3 days He will rise.*

Second Statement: Read Matthew 17:22–23 (Mark 9:30–32; Luke 9:43–45).

4. What do the disciples learn about His death from His *second* prophecy? *He will be betrayed by one of them. On 3rd day he will arise.*

Luke adds a few interesting emotional elements to the story.

> *And they were all amazed at the greatness of God. While everyone was marveling at all that Jesus did, he said to his disciples, "Listen carefully to what I am about to tell you: The Son of Man is going to be betrayed into the hands of men." But they did not understand what this meant. It was hidden from them, so that they did not grasp it, and they were afraid to ask him about it. (Luke 9:43–45)*

> They were on their way up to Jerusalem, with Jesus leading the way, and the disciples were astonished, while those who followed were afraid. Again he took the Twelve aside and told them what was going to happen to him. (Mark 10:32)

Third Statement: Read Luke 18:31–34 (Matthew 20:17–19; Mark 10:32–34).

5. What new information does Luke give us about this third prediction? *All the predictions of the prophets will be fulfilled + come true. He will be betrayed to the leading priests & teachers of the law who will sentence Him to die; be flogged by the Romans & then crucified. Will arise on 3rd day.*

6. Put a check by the facts the disciples have been told.

- ☑ The Son of Man will be betrayed.
- ☑ Jesus will be rejected and suffer many things at the hands of religious leaders.
- ☑ The Son of Man will be handed over to the Gentiles.
- ☑ The Gentiles will mock, insult, spit, and flog him.
- ☑ The Son of Man will be condemned to death.
- ☑ The Son of Man will be lifted up from the earth.
- ☑ Jesus must be killed.
- ☑ Jesus will be raised to life on the third day.
- ☑ The Son of Man will come in His Father's glory and reward each man's work.

The answer is: all of the above. Jesus is so specific in these passages. And the fulfillment of the persecution passages is so deadly accurate. Why don't they believe He will rise again? Bible commentator Matthew Henry writes,

> The disciples' prejudices were so strong, that they would not understand these things literally. They were so intent upon the prophecies which spake of

Christ's glory, that they overlooked those which spake of his sufferings. People run into mistakes, because they read their Bibles by halves, and are only for the smooth things. We are as backward to learn the proper lessons from the sufferings, crucifixion, and resurrection of Christ, as the disciples were to what he told them as to those events; and for the same reason; self-love, and a desire of worldly objects, close our understandings.[18]

Jesus' Words in Action: Jim Elliot, missionary to the Auca Indians in Ecuador, wrote in his journal, "He is no fool who gives what he cannot keep to gain what he cannot lose."

Jim Elliot couldn't have known then that in six years he would be murdered by the very people he was trying to save. After his death, his wife and others continued ministering to his murderers, and many came to salvation in Christ. His life is now the subject of books and a movie.

> *I tell you the truth, unless a kernel of wheat falls to the ground and dies, it remains only a single seed. But if it dies, it produces many seeds. The man who loves his life will lose it, while the man who hates his life in this world will keep it for eternal life. (John 12:24–25)*

As followers of Christ, we will share in His suffering as well as His glory. Jesus' words from His sermon on the Mount remind us of this:

> *Blessed are those who are persecuted because of righteousness, or theirs is the kingdom of heaven. Blessed are you when people insult you, persecute you and falsely say all kinds of evil against you because of me. Rejoice and be glad, because great is your reward in heaven, for in the same way they persecuted the prophets who were before you. (Matthew 5:10-12)*

It's a challenge, but remember you are BLESSED, and rejoice!

> "The man who loves his life will lose it, while the man who hates his life in this world will keep it for eternal life." (John 12:25)
>
>

Works Cited

1. Maier, Paul L., *In the Fullness of Time: A Historian Looks at Christmas, Easter, and the Early Church* (Grand Rapids, MI: Kregel, 1991), 108.

2. *The MacArthur Study Bible* (Nashville, TN: Thomas Nelson, Word Publishing, 1997), 1554.

3. Ray Vander Laan and Focus on the Family Video (That the World May Know Series), *The True Easter Story and Lamb of God* (Grand Rapids, MI: Zondervan, 2000); Maier, 108.

4. Vander Laan and Focus on the Family Video, *The True Easter Story and Lamb of God.* "Messiah in Passover," http://biblicalholidays.com

5. Vander Laan and Focus on the Family Video, *The True Easter Story and Lamb of God.*

6. Deffinbaugh, Bob, "The Untriumphal Entry (Luke 19:28–44)," http://www.bible.org.

7. *The MacArthur Study Bible,* 1484.

8. Deffinbaugh, "The Triumphal Tragedy," http://www.bible.org.

9. *Harper's Bible Commentary,* in Accordance Bible software. CD-ROM, version 5.7. Oak Tree Software, Inc.
Easton's Bible Dictionary, in Accordance Bible software. CD-ROM, version 5.7. Oak Tree Software, Inc.

10. Vander Laan and Focus on the Family Video, *The True Easter Story and Lamb of God.*
Deffinbaugh, "The Untriumphal Entry (Luke 19:28–44), http://www.bible.org.

11. Vander Laan and Focus on the Family Video, *The True Easter Story and Lamb of God.*

12. Lucado, Max, *The Final Week of Jesus* (Multnomah, OR: Multnomah Books, 1994), 21.

13. Ibid.

14. Bishop, Jim, *The Day Christ Died: The Inspiring Classic on the Last 24 Hours of Jesus' Life* (San Francisco: Harper, 1957), 55.

15. Ibid.

16. MacArthur, John, *The Murder of Jesus: A Study of How Jesus Died* (Nashville, TN: Thomas Nelson, 2000), 106–107.

17. Vander Laan and Focus on the Family Video (That the World May Know Series), *Faith Lessons on the Death and Resurrection of the Messiah: City of a Great King (1)* (Grand Rapids, MI: Zondervan, 1997, 1998), Volume 4, Video 1.
Deffinbaugh, "The Tempest in the Temple: The Abuses of Authority" (Luke 20:1–18), http://www.bible.org.
———, "The Triumphal Tragedy" (Mark 11:1–25), http://www.bible.org.

18. *Matthew Henry Commentary,* in Accordance Bible software. CD-ROM, version 5.7. Oak Tree Software, Inc.

WEEK SIX

Passion Week

The Last Days

Last week we saw Jesus enter Jerusalem with the Passover lambs as *the* Passover Lamb. Today we look back to see His significance as the *Lamb of God.*

Monday: The Significance of the Lamb

The Lord promised the Hebrews freedom from their Egyptian bondage (Exodus 6:6–8).

Moses pleaded with Pharaoh to "Let my people go," but Pharaoh refused. After nine plagues that afflicted the Egyptians with bloody waters, frogs, lice, flies, disease, boils, a hailstorm, locusts, and darkness, God chose to kill all the first-born sons in Egypt while *passing over* the Israelites.

📖 Read Exodus 12:21–23 below to discover the origin of Passover.

> "We all, like sheep, have gone astray, each of us has turned to his own way; and the LORD has laid on him the iniquity of us all." (Isaiah 53:6)

> *Then Moses summoned all the elders of Israel and said to them, "Go at once and select the animals for your families and slaughter the Passover lamb. Take a bunch of hyssop, dip it into the blood in the basin and put some of the blood on the top and on both sides of the doorframe. None of you shall go out of the door of your house until morning. When the LORD goes through the land to strike down the Egyptians, he will see the blood on the top and sides of the doorframe and will pass over that doorway, and he will not permit the destroyer to enter your houses and strike you down.*

1. Did God really need a marking on a door to let Him know where the Israelites lived? Of course He didn't. So why do you think God required this sign? *He wanted the Hebrews to recognize his protection*

2. According to Exodus 12:5, the animals chosen must be

_____.

We own a sheep farm that has provided me with insight about Passover. I'll share three lessons in today's study.

One year my sensitive first grader grieved the death of a struggling lamb. With tears in her eyes, Julia begged me for an answer. "Why did it have to die? It didn't do *anything* wrong!" I agreed with her. It seemed very unfair; the lamb had done nothing wrong. Neither had Jesus. He was the perfect, spotless, sinless lamb—who did absolutely nothing wrong. It took a perfect lamb to take away the sins of the world.

3. How long was the sacrificial lamb to live with the family (Exodus 12:3, 6)? Why were these days required? *(not)*
14th day of 1st mo. @ twilight. So that the family would hold it as special.

Old Testament Prophecy Fulfilled

"The next day John saw Jesus coming toward him and said, 'Look, the Lamb of God, who takes away the sin of the world!'" (John 1:29)

The Passover lamb was chosen on the tenth day of the Hebrew month, *Nisan,* and it was slain on the fourteenth day. Between those days, the Passover lamb was kept and cared for in the house. Perhaps this made the sacrifice more difficult for the family. My experience has formed my opinion that few baby animals are as sweet as young lambs.

After the mother ewe has cleaned her lamb, the young lamb stands on knobby knees and attempts to nurse. However, sometimes a lamb is weak or cold or the mother cannot care for it. On these occasions, we warm the lamb in a lukewarm bath, blow-dry it, wrap it in a towel, and keep it in a warm place until we can return it to its mother. If the mother has died or rejects the lamb, the lamb becomes a bottle feeder. My daughters have taken bottle feeders to school for show-and-tell. They become like cherished pets. My husband discourages us from naming the sheep, because every named animal becomes special and painful to send to market. We usually try to give away our bottle feeders to friends who want a pet lamb. This avoids grief on market day when my daughters would have to say goodbye to a lamb we've bottle-fed four to six times a day for six weeks. How difficult it must have been to sacrifice that chosen lamb at Passover. It had a name—the name of the family for whom it was sacrificed.

4. What time of day was the animal to be slaughtered (12:6)?
Twilight.

5. What else was to be included in the dinner for this celebration (Exodus 12:8)? *With bitter Stalk greens + unleaven bread*

When Julia was a toddler, she pointed to one lambie and said, "Mommy, that one doesn't have its price tag!" I laughed, because none of them had a "price tag"! They had *ear tags*. But it made me think. Jesus the Lamb of God had a huge price tag on Him. No one could ever determine the infinite value of saving all the believers for eternity. The price was His life, a huge cost. How much would you pay for eternity? Infinite value, and yet it's free for the asking.

Over a thousand years later, the celebration of Passover continued. Let's see what it looked like in Jesus' time.

Christ's sacrifice on the cross as the *Lamb of God* has made the *Passover* Lamb forever unnecessary. Bible Commentator Matthew Henry encourages us to spend all of our days remembering God's work through the ages and finds the *last* Passover a more important night than the *first*. "Then a yoke, heavier than that of Egypt, was broken from off our necks, and a land, better than that of Canaan, set before us. It was a redemption to be celebrated in heaven, for ever and ever."[1]

> For you know that it was not with perishable things such as silver or gold that you were redeemed from the empty way of life handed down to you from your forefathers, but with the precious blood of Christ, a lamb without blemish or defect (1 Peter 1:18–19).

Jesus' Words in Action: God put a priority on remembering and celebrating freedom. Celebrate what God has done. List the miracles. Re-tell the stories of God's faithfulness to you and your family.[2]

> Christ's final passover introduces the first Lord's Supper

Tuesday: The Last Passover

How many times have we experienced the Lord's Supper and heard the familiar words, "This is my blood of the covenant, which is poured out for many" (Mark 14:24)? Today, pretend it is the very *first* time you heard those words and witness this *Last Passover* for the *first* time.

Jesus asks His disciples to prepare for a Passover to end all Passovers—literally. For Christians, Passover becomes the *Last* Supper to be replaced by the *Lord's* Supper.

[handwritten top margin:] Women usually carried water, not men. So he would have stood out. This one 1st day of Festival of Unleavened bread.

[handwritten left margin:] MATT. Mark does mention man carrying water. The met them on the way to the city. They accosted him instead of following him. Mark The room was already set up.

Read Luke 22:7–13 (compare to Matthew 26:17–19; Mark 14:12–16).

1. Who are the only individuals "in the know"? Why do you think the other disciples are not given these directions? *The man that followed + Jesus.*

Finding the location is simplified because women usually carry the water. Peter and John's responsibilities include securing a lamb between the ages of eight days and one year, purchasing herbs, spices, and bread, cleansing the home of leaven, cooking unleavened bread, and sacrificing the lamb, like every Jewish male does within a fifteen-mile radius around Jerusalem.[3] For the Passover celebration, circa AD 30, the *shofar* is blown at 3:00 p.m., when lambs are sacrificed. The sacrifices continue until 5:00 p.m. (twilight). If everyone in these regions observed Passover the same way, then nearly a quarter of a million lambs would have to be slain in two hours. That would necessitate six hundred priests killing four lambs per minute. However, certain regions celebrate Passover from sunrise to sunrise, and others from sundown to sundown, which spreads out the sacrificing to two days[4] and allows Jesus to both *celebrate* Passover as well as *to offer Himself as* the Passover Lamb.[5]

Read John 13:1–11 (The washing of the disciples' feet).

2. John 13:3 states: "Jesus knew that the Father had put *all things* under *His hands*, and that he had come from *God* and was returning to *God*;"

3. Then verse 4 continues with "*SO he got up from the meal. . . .*" Why the connection? *After the meal, he washed their feet.*

Washing feet was customary; the lowest slaves were asked (though they could not be commanded) to do this job.[6]

4. What happens if Peter is not washed (verse 8)? *If I do not wash you, you have no part with me.*

5. How does Jesus show the full extent of His love? *By becoming a SERVANT.*

6. Read Mark 14:18–21 (also Matthew 26:21–25; Luke 22:21–23). Who asks if they might be the betrayer (Mark 14:19)? *Each one asked.*

Can you imagine how you might feel if your fingers were in the bowl at the moment Jesus said, "one who dips bread into the bowl with me?" (Mark 14:21)

"For even the Son of Man did not come to be served, but to serve, and to give his life as a ransom for many." (Mark 10:45)

After the third cup, the cup of redemption, Jesus inserts something new into the familiar Passover ceremony, and this is a surprise to the disciples.

📖 Read Luke 22:17–20—The Lord's Supper (Matthew 26:26–29, Mark 14:22–25).

In the middle of this Passover Feast known as the Last Supper, after taking a cup and giving thanks, Jesus introduces a "new covenant." According to Ray Vander Laan's *That the World May Know* video series, engagement and marriage feasts during Christ's time contained references to a "new covenant." After the bride price has been negotiated by both sets of parents, a cup of wine is poured for the son. The son then offers the cup to his bride-to-be and asks her to accept his "new covenant" represented in the marriage agreement terms. Drinking from the cup symbolized the bride's formal acceptance of the marriage proposal and all the good and bad circumstances that come with marriage. According to Vander Laan, when Christ mentions "a new covenant" during this Passover occasion, the disciples most likely associated these three words with the wedding customs of the times. Through the illustration of a man's love and devotion for his bride, they gained at least a nebulous comprehension of Christ's unswerving love and devotion for them and for all who follow Him.[7]

> **Old Testament Prophecy Fulfilled**
>
> "Even my close friend, whom I trusted, he who shared my bread, has lifted up his heel against me." (Psalms 41:9)

> "This is my blood of the covenant, which is poured out for many." (Mark 14:24)

📖 Read Luke 22:24–38.

After the disciples bicker about who is greatest, Jesus says, (fill in the blanks below)?

7. "The *greatest* among you should be like the *least*, and the one who *leads* like the one who *serves*. For who is *important*, the one who is at the *table* or the one who *serving*? Is it not the one who is at the table? But I am among you as the one who *serves*" (Luke 22:26–27).

8. How do His actions mirror His words? *He served them.*

Jesus' Words in Action: The next time you celebrate communion, remember you are the *bride of Christ*. What a beautiful description! As the bride of Christ, we long for the Bridegroom's return. And in the meantime, we consider service for Him that involves our words and our actions.

Wednesday: P.S., I Love You.

It is nearly time for Jesus to say goodbye to His disciples. Listen for His love and fatherly caring. He will call them *my children* and assure them that He will not leave them as orphans. Oh, how great is His love, and how He longs for them to be unified in love.

📖 Read John 13:30–38; 14:1–27.

1. Fill in the words from scripture. "A new command I give to you: _love_ one another. As I have _loved_ you, so you must _love_ _one_ _another_. By this _all_ ____ will know that you are my _disciples_, if you _love_ one another" (John 13:34–35).

2. In these final moments, Peter, Thomas, Philip, and Judas have some individual questions (13:36–37, 14:5, 14:8, 14:22). In your own words, write each man's questions, and then add your own question. What might *you* have asked? Has Jesus answered your question? *Jesus, how will I recognize the Holy Spirit's work in me?*

As He did during the Passover meal, Jesus uses verbiage from the betrothal ceremony. After the groom offers the cup to the bride and she accepts the cup, he says he will go and prepare a place for her by adding rooms onto his father's home. This betrothal time could last up to twelve months. When the father feels the home is ready, he alerts the son to go to his bride. The wedding party, including the bridesmaids with their lamps full of oil, proceeds to the home of the bride. When the "best man" announces their arrival with the blowing of the shofar, the bride dresses for the occasion and runs to greet her groom.[8]

Jesus uses the marriage picture to depict what is happening at His departure. He's readying heaven for believers on earth. He leaves to prepare a place for us, but He will return. Will our lamps be burning? Will we run to greet our Bridegroom?

Thursday: The Holy Spirit

Jesus' final words continue to offer comfort and a Comforter. He also makes it clear how to join His Father.

Remember the I AM statements? They are about to reappear.

> "In my Father's house are many rooms; if it were not so, I would have told you. I am going there to prepare a place for you. And if I go and prepare a place for you, I will come back and take you to be with me that you also may be where I am." (John 14:2–3)

Handwritten marginalia:

Phillip: Lord, show us the F. "It is sufficient for us." "Have I been you so long & yet you have not known? He who has seen the F."

Judas: How is it that you will manifest yourself to us, & not to the world? The Helper, the Holy Spirit, whom the Father will send in my name, He will teach you all things, & help you to remember what I have said.

Peter: Lord, where are you going. "Where I am going you cannot follow me now." But you will follow me later.

Thomas: How will we know the way. "I am the way, the truth, & the life. No one comes to the F except through me."

📖 Read John 14:1–15.

1. Fill in the blanks below:

"I am the _way_ and the _truth_ and the _life_. _No_ _one_ comes to the _Father_ except through _me_. If you really _know_ me, you would _know_ my _Father_ as well. From now on, you do _know_ him and have _seen_ him." (John 14:5–7)

Many people want to believe that all religions lead to God. But Jesus claims there is NO way to the Father except *through* Him. If we believe in Jesus and His words, we cannot be vague about the one way to salvation. He wouldn't have needed to die on the cross if there were many other ways.

📖 Read John 14:16–21 below.

And I will ask the Father, and he will give you another advocate to help you and be with you forever—the Spirit of truth. The world cannot accept him, because it neither sees him nor knows him. But you know him, for he lives with you and will be in you. I will not leave you as orphans; I will come to you. Before long, the world will not see me anymore, but you will see me. Because I live, you also will live. On that day you will realize that I am in my Father, and you are in me, and I am in you. Whoever has my commands and keeps them is the one who loves me. The one who loves me will be loved by my Father, and I too will love them and show myself to them.*

2. Underline what you find comforting in His words to His followers in the Scripture passage above. How is Jesus Father-like? *He wants us to be known to Him* *ees to Him. He gives us* *commands to follow to show our love for Him. in our obedience.*

3. Jesus continues to comfort as a father. Memorize this next verse, and recall it the next time your heart is anxious.

"_Peace_ I leave with you; my _peace_ I give you. I do not give to you as the world gives. Do not let your hearts be _troubled_ and do not be _afraid_." (John 14:27)

📖 Read John 14:28–31.

Jesus says, "Come now; let us leave" (verse 31). He knows what's coming, but His followers cannot even comprehend. Jesus leaves the communion of friends to journey to where they will desert Him. This is the beginning of the end.

Jesus' Words in Action: Jesus' final messages are about peace ("Peace I leave with you") and love ("Love one another"). How can we reach out with unconditional and sacrificial love so others will know we are Christians by our love? *By just showing that love for God.*

The Drama of the Passion

Gethsemane to Golgotha in 13 Scenes

Scene One

Title: The sheep and the rooster
Reference: *Matthew 26:30–35*
Location: *Walking to Mount of Olives*
Characters: *Jesus, disciples (not Judas)*

Scene Two

Title: Jesus' last words and prayers
References: *John 15, 16, 17*
Scene: *Walking to Kidron Valley*
Characters: *Jesus, disciples, (not Judas)*

Scene Three

Title: Jesus prays/disciples sleep
Reference: *Mark 14:32–42*
  (Matthew 26:36–46; Luke 22:40–46)
Location: *Gethsemane: Olive grove*
Characters: *Jesus, Peter, James, John*

Scene Four

Title: Jesus is arrested
Reference: *John 18:2–12*
  (Matthew 26:47–56; Mark 14:43–49; Luke 22:47–54)
Location: *Gethsemane: Olive grove*
Characters: *Jesus, disciples, Roman soldiers, Jewish officials, Malchus, Judas*

? *Malchus, Judas*

The High Priests plan.

Scene Five (Religious Trial #1)

Title: Jesus before Annas
Reference: *John 18:12b–24*
Location: *Home of Annas/Courtyard*
Characters: *Jesus, Annas, members of Sanhedrin, John, Peter, servant girl*
*Meanwhile, Peter denies Jesus the first time

Scene Six (Religious Trial #2)

Title: "I AM" before Caiaphas
Reference: *Mark 14:55–65*
  (Matt 26:59–68; Luke 22:63–65)
Location: *Home of Caiaphas/ Courtyard*
Characters: *Jesus, chief priests, Sanhedrin, guards, Peter*
**Meanwhile Peter denies Jesus the second time (Matthew 26:69–72; Luke 22:55–58)
***Peter denies Jesus the 3rd time (Luke 22:59–62)
(Matthew 26:73–75; Mark 14:70b–72; John 18:26–27)

Scene Seven (Religious Trial #3)

Title: "I AM" before the council
Reference: *Luke 22:66–71*
Location: *Perhaps high priests' home*
Characters: *Jesus, council of the elders, chief priests, teachers of the law*
**Judas remorsefully returns to chief priests (Matthew 27:3–10)

Scene Eight A (Political Trial #1)

Title: Jesus before Pilate
Reference: ***John 18:28–32***
              (Matthew 27:2; Luke 23:1–2)
Location: *Outside Praetorium*
Characters: *Pilate and the Jews*

Scene Eight B

Title: The King before Pilate
Reference: ***John 18:33–38***
              (Matthew 27:11–14;
              Mark 15:2–5; Luke
              23:3,4)
Location: *Inside/Outside Praetorium*
Characters: *Jesus, Pilate, Jews*

Scene Nine (Political Trial #2)

Title: Jesus before Herod
Reference: ***Luke 23:5–12***
Location: *Herod's Palace*
Characters: *Jesus, Herod, chief priests,*
              teachers of the law, soldiers

Scene Ten (Political Trial #3)

Title: Jesus or Barabbas?
References: ***Luke 23:13–16, Mark***
              15:6–14
              (Matthew 27:15–23; John
              18:39–40)
Location: *Praetorium*
Characters: *Jesus, Barabbas, Pilate,*
              chief priests, crowd
**Pilate's wife sends Pilate a
concerned warning (Matthew 27:19)

Scene Eleven

Title: Jesus is persecuted.
Reference: ***Matthew 27:27–30***
              (John 19:1–3; Mark
              15:16–19)
Location: *Praetorium*
Characters: *Jesus, Pilate, governor's soldiers*

Scene Twelve

Title: "Crucify! Crucify!
Reference: ***John 19:4–17***
              (Matthew 27:24–26, 31;
              Luke 23:24–25)
Location: *Inside/Outside Praetorium*
Characters: *Jesus, crowd, Pilate, chief*
              priests, Barabas

Scene Thirteen

Title: Journey to the Cross
Reference: ***Luke 23:26–31; Mark***
              15:21–22
Location: *Way of Sorrows*
Characters: *Jesus, women, crowd, soldiers, Simon of Cyrene*

Friday: The Garden of Gethsemane

Max Lucado writes in *The Final Week of Jesus*, "The final battle was won in Gethsemane. . . . For it was in the garden that he made his decision. He would rather go to hell for you than go to heaven without you."[9]

Look at the chart on pages 96–97 where you will find the final scenes of Jesus' life depicted in **The Drama of the Passion: Gethsemane to Golgotha in 13 Scenes.** This is your road map complete with location, characters, and references. For the next few days you will refer to these pages and read the bold references to better understand the sequence of events.

Now let's walk from Jerusalem to the Mount of Olives. To get there, we will have to cross the Kidron Valley. The moon is full and illuminates the Kidron Brook, which is red with the sacrificial blood of at least a hundred thousand Passover Lambs flowing from the altar down a strait to the brook.[10] What is going through Jesus' mind with that visual reminder of sacrifice?

Today you'll be reading four sections of scripture to absorb the final moments before Jesus' arrest.

📖 Read Matthew 26:30–35, the reference for **Scene 1** from the Drama of the Passion flow chart.

As the disciples travel to the Mount of Olives, they sing a hymn (see Mark 14:26). The chosen hymn might have been from Psalms 115—118 because of its connection with the Passover.

Scene Two is when Jesus and his disciples walk to the Kidron Valley. This is one of my favorite scenes in the Bible. These are Jesus' last words to His disciples before His arrest and were meant to last. These instructions are full of metaphors. In this section, Jesus explains that He is the vine and we are the branches and teaches about love.

He last spoke of love and peace. Now He'll talk about joy.

📖 Skim-Read John 15:1–16.

1. Draw a sketch of John 15:5. Jesus obeyed His Father's commands and remained in His love (John 15:10).

2. Fill in the blanks. "We are to _obey_ Jesus' commands and to _remain_ in His love so that His _love_ may be in us and our _joy_ will be _full_." (John 15:10–11)

3. Write John 15:18–19 in your own words so that you can apply it today. *Do not worry if the world hates you, It hated Jesus as well. You are not like them so they naturally hate you.*

The disciples are clueless about Jesus' departure (John 16:16–18). He compares the separation and reunion to the pain of childbirth (John 16:19–24)! Though it's hard to imagine my husband understanding what it felt like to deliver our girls, when my daughter asks, "Did it hurt?" I can honestly say, "I'd do it tomorrow for another baby!" We rejoice in the new life we have in Christ as we do with a new life in our family.

📖 Skim-read John 17 (conclusion of **Scene 2**) You get to witness Jesus' prayer to His Father. He prays for His disciples, and then He prays for YOU.[11] Read verses 20–21 of John 17 below.

> "I have told you these things, so that in me you may have peace. In this world you will have trouble. But take heart! I have overcome the world." (John 16:33)

"My prayer is not for them alone. I pray also for those who will believe in me through their message, that all of them may be one, Father, just as you are in me and I am in you.

📖 Read Mark 14:32–42 **(Scene Three),** your final reading for the day!

Jesus prays in the Garden of Gethsemane, a garden of olive trees. The word "Gethsemane" means "olive press." While in the garden, Jesus Himself is pressed so hard by anxiety and fear that His capillaries burst and he excretes blood in His sweat, a condition known as hematridosis. Isn't it interesting that it is Dr. Luke who mentions it in Luke 22:44?[12]

> "And now, Father, glorify me in your presence with the glory I had with you before the world began." (John 17:5)

John MacArthur in *The Murder of Jesus* answers that question this way. "Clearly, what Christ dreaded most about the cross—the cup from which He asks to be delivered if possible—was the outpouring of divine wrath He would have to endure from His holy Father."[13] MacArthur further describes this scene as one of *sorrow, supplication and submission.*[14]

Jesus chose to drink of the cup. He prayed for *you* and drank the cup for *you* knowing everything you have done and will do in your life. What undying love He exhibits while under pressure in the Garden!

Jesus' Words in Action: What do you learn from Jesus about the importance of prayer? How do you feel knowing He prayed for you? His longing to pray for you and to talk to His Father indicates His desire for relationship. How does this motivate you? *Since it was God's will that Jesus complete the plan, I can only assume Jesus prayed for the strength to endure. That He prayed for me then motivates me to abide in Him.*

> "Watch and pray so that you will not fall into temptation. The spirit is willing, but the body is weak." (Matthew 26:41)

Works Cited

1. *Matthew Henry Commentary*, in Accordance Bible software. CD-ROM, version 5.7. Oak Tree Software, Inc.

2. Gariepy, Henry, *40 Days with the Savior: Preparing Your Heart for Easter, Meditations on the Final Days and Suffering of Our Lord* (Nashville: TN: Thomas Nelson, 1995), 40–41.

3. Bishop, Jim, *The Day Christ Died: The Inspiring Classic on the Last 24 Hours of Jesus' Life* (San Francisco: Harper, 1957), 7, 18–19.

MacArthur, John, *The Murder of Jesus: A Study of How Jesus Died* (Nashville, TN: Thomas Nelson, 2000), 26.

4. MacArthur, 26.

5. Deffinbaugh, Th.M, "The Passover Plan: Man Proposes, God Disposes," http://www.bible.org.

The MacArthur Study Bible, (Nashville, TN: Thomas Nelson, Word Publishing, 1997), 1571.

6. Deffinbaugh, Th.M, "The Last Supper (Luke 22:1–23)" http://www.bible.org.

7. Ray Vander Laan and Focus on the Family Video (That the World May Know Series), *The True Easter Story, That the World May Know* (Grand Rapids, MI: Zondervan, 2000.

8. http://www.familybible.org/FAQ/Baptism.html
http://www.biblestudymanuals.net/jewish marriage customs.html

9. Lucado, Max, *The Final Week of Jesus* (Multnomah: Multnomah Books, 1994), 94.

10. MacArthur, *The Murder of Jesus: A Study of How Jesus Died*, 47. Gariepy, 43.

11. Lucado, 92–94.

12. Zugibe, Frederick, *The Cross and the Shroud: A Medical Inquiry into the Crucifixion* (New York: Paragon House, 1988), 3.

Bishop, Jim, *The Day Christ Died: The Inspiring Classic on the Last 24 Hours of Jesus' Life* (San Francisco: Harper, 1957), 169.

13. MacArthur, 69.

14. Vander Laan and Focus on the Family Video (That the World May Know Series), *Faith Lessons on the Death and Resurrection of the Messiah: The Weight of the World* (Grand Rapids, MI: Zondervan, 1997, 1998) Volume 4, Video 2.

The Way of Sorrow

Monday: When Jesus Looks at You

Have you ever disappointed someone? Failed them? As a mom, you know that when your children make a mistake, you still love them. Jesus' disciples have failed Him. Two have betrayed or denied Him. What will happen?

Today we will read scenes four through seven and move from Jesus' arrest to His trials by the religious leaders. For each scene, place yourself there with Jesus and the other characters.

I.N.R.I.
Iesus Nazarenus Rex Iudaeorum

(Latin abbreviation for Jesus of Nazareth, the King of the Jews)

Place bookmarks at John 18, Mark 14, Luke 22. Or type each reference into a Bible app such as BibleGateway to make your studying easier. This is a difficult week emotionally. Prepare to walk with Jesus through a week of betrayal, pain, and suffering. It was all for you.

Read John 18:2–12 (**Scene Four**).

1. Who shows up to arrest Jesus (verses 2–3)? *leading priests, Pharisees, Judas, Roman soldiers + temple guards; Simon Peter, Malchus (High priests slave)*

2. What literally knocks the soldiers off their feet (John 18:6)? Why are those words powerful? *They were startled by His boldness or by the words "I AM he," a declaration of divinity; or by His obvious power/authority.*

Somehow the divine authority + power of Jesus was revealed to these armed men, causing them to fall down in fear, panic + awe.

In Matthew 26:53, Jesus explains He could have called on twelve legions of angels. Since a legion equals six thousand soldiers, this means seventy-two thousand angels![1] God's army is a lot bigger than any human army, but Jesus doesn't intend to do battle with clubs and swords. Jesus came in peace, as we will see with His healing in the Garden (Luke 22:51).

One year I witnessed the Garden of Gethsemane scene in our local Passion Play from a new and profound perspective. The play depicts Jesus praying, the soldiers and religious leaders arriving to arrest Jesus, and then Peter cutting off the slave Malchus' ear.

My seven-year-old nephew, Tim, came with us and ran from scene to scene, wriggling to the front to catch all the action. Now at the Garden, I could see Jesus and the servant, as well as my nephew wearing his ear-cap to protect his ear after his most recent surgery.

When Tim was born, I had watched the birth video and how the nurse gently explained to his adoring first-time parents that Tim's ear was deformed. Tim had a miniature ear with no hole. With medical advances in hearing repair, my brother and his wife opted for Tim to have multiple surgeries. Doctors created an ear from skin and cartilage from other areas on his body, and they would one day drill a hole in his skull.

Tim focused on the servant's bloodied ear and the gentle Jesus. I will never forget Tim's look of awe and surprised joy as He watched Jesus heal the servant, Jesus' last miracle before the miracle of the cross. With a slow realization, Tim connected with that wounded youth as well as the gentle and healing Jesus who came to bring peace, not the sword. Can you, too, connect with the Healer in the Garden?

By the end of the scene, Jesus is alone. This evening began with lessons of love and unselfish actions and now concludes with all the disciples fleeing and deserting Christ (see Matthew 26:56b). Have you ever been ignored or betrayed? Can you even begin to imagine what it would feel like to have your closest friends desert you? At some point Peter and another disciple get up enough nerve to follow Jesus and his captors to find out what is happening to their Lord (John 18:15). This takes us to the beginning of His religious trials and scenes 5, 6, and 7.

Read John 18:12b–24 (**Scene Five**).

Caiaphas and Annas direct the religious trials. As in-laws and religious leaders, they probably live in the same large facility, their rooms separated by a courtyard.[2] They also share a problem: they want Jesus sentenced to death for blasphemy, but the Romans won't execute a person for those reasons alone. However, Romans will execute for sedition or insurrection.[3] Now the religious leaders need to make the crime fit the punishment of death.

> "Why do the nations conspire and the peoples plot in vain? The kings of the earth take their stand and the rulers gather together agains the Lord and against his Anointed One." (Psalm 2:1–2)

Jesus will endure six trials, three by religious leaders and three by political leaders.[4] In these trials, almost all the rules will be broken. Truly, this should have been a mistrial except that nothing is a mistake with God.

Consider these rules as you watch Jesus undergo the trials:

- No night arrests or night trials
- Trials should recess until morning
- No trials on Feast Days or the Sabbath
- Trials should be held in Hall of Hewn Stone—Temple (not High Priests' residence)
- Trials must be public
- The accused should be considered innocent until proven guilty
- Must be indicted before arraigned (i.e., formally charged before being brought to court)
- Charges must be brought from *outside* the council
- The accused must have representation/defense, witnesses, and evidence
- The accused must not be hit or spat upon
- Witnesses must have precise testimony, dates, times, locations
- False witnesses could receive the death sentence
- Trial should last 2–3 days and include fasting
- If condemned, *must* be a *two-day* trial, and *must* have a re-vote[5]

As we look at **Scenes 5, 6**, and **7**, let's also follow Peter and Judas. If I were directing a stage production of these events, I'd have the curtain closed and Peter's first two denials occur in front of the curtain while the set changes to Caiaphas' room. Peter would be questioned and deny knowing the Messiah. At last, he would flee off stage and we'd open to the next scene with Caiaphas, Jesus, and the Sanhedrin, which is what we'll examine right now.

Read Mark 14:55–65 (**Scene Six— Religious Trial #2**).

When Jesus is asked if He is the Christ, and the Son of the Blessed One, Jesus responds, "*I am.*" When Jesus claims to be the One prophesied in Daniel 7:13–14, the high priest goes berserk. What about the high priest's meltdown and drama-king

> "The high priest, the one among his brothers who has had the anointing oil poured on his head and who has been ordained to wear the priestly garments, must not let his hair become unkempt or tear his clothes." (Leviticus 21:10)

The religious leaders + Pharisees would have been familiar c Daniel passage

Daniel; "as my vision continued that night, I saw someone like the son of man coming with the clouds of Heaven. He approached the ancient one was led into His presence. He was given authority, honor + sovereignty over all nations so the people..."

maneuver? According to Leviticus 21:10, he isn't supposed to do that.[6] But then again, nobody in this trial proceeding is doing anything the way it is supposed to be done.

The High Priest has the highest rank of all the priests... he has been ordained to wear priestly garments. He must never leave his hair uncombed or tear his clothing.

📖 Read Luke 22:66–71 (**Scene Seven**).

Perhaps one of the most horrendous scenes in the Bible is when a high priest's servant (a relative of the man Peter cut) recognizes Peter's involvement and accuses Peter. As a tortured Jesus is taken from one room to another, Peter denies Jesus in Jesus' presence. Read the verse in the margin.

Peter sees a beaten, interrogated man who loves Him more than anyone in the world. That man looks deep into his eyes and soul at the moment Peter denies Him.[7] What did those eyes look like? Will Peter ever forget them?

In various scenes, Luke is the writer who captures Peter's reactions. In Luke 22:54 we learn that when Jesus is arrested, Peter follows at a distance, and after His denial with Jesus watching, Luke reveals that Peter "went outside and wept bitterly" (Luke 22:62).

> "The Lord turned and looked straight at Peter. Then Peter remembered the word the Lord had spoken to him: 'Before the rooster crows today, you will disown me three times.'" (Matthew 22:61) 🌿✝️

For a minute, pretend that you're Peter. We've all denied the Lord, we've all sinned, and we've all chosen the sword instead of peace. What if every time we did something wrong we saw the disappointed face of Jesus? What if the Holy Spirit crowed a warning for us, and we allowed ourselves to hear it?

As we move closer to the cross, will you remember that Christ knew the cup He was accepting, and that He accepted this cup for you? He already knew everything you were going to do, and He still went to the cross.

Jesus' Words in Action: At an Easter retreat, I asked each woman to draw a picture of herself at the cross or write words that could later become a poem or a song. A woman named Molly was gripped by Jesus' look at Peter. Because of her background, she had always assumed it was a look of condemnation. She now realized it had to be a look of *undying love*. She wrote,

Peter, I loved you before you were born,
I see you as I created you to be,
knowing your heart will turn back to me,
    the Lamb of God,
who came to die to set you free
from the condemnation that will crucify me.

Molly died young from a brain tumor but has now seen Jesus and and experienced His loving look.

What kind of look motivates? A look of undying love. When disciplining children, what kind of a look do you give them? How does Peter react to this undying and sacrificial love? We learn through Scripture that Peter goes on to be one of Jesus' most devout followers. Today, let's remember the loving look of Jesus.

Tuesday: Pilate and Politics

📖 Read John 18:28–32 (**Scene Eight**).

Pilate has to come *outside* to address the crowd because the Jews cannot enter the home of a non-Jew or they will defile themselves for Friday's Passover.[8]

Though Jewish leaders considered blasphemy to be a crime punishable by death, the Romans did not. The Jewish death penalty was carried out by stoning, but according to prophecy, Jesus had to be lifted up. Do you see the problem?

📖 Read John 18:33–38 (**Scene Eight B**).

1. In your own words, write Jesus' responses to Pilate's statements (verses 34, 36, 37).

Pilate's statement:	Jesus' Answer:
1. Are you the king of the Jews?	*Did you draw this conclusion*
2. What is it you have done?	*No kingdom is of this world.*
3. You are a king!	*I was born to testify of the truth.*
4. What is truth?	*Everyone who listened to Jesus.*

📖 Read Luke 23:5–12 (**Scene Nine**).

Pilate wants out of the Jesus mess, so he passes Jesus off to Herod, since Jesus is from Herod's political region.

Herod must be shocked when He sees Jesus. MacArthur describes,

> How different Christ must have looked from the strong, prophetic miracle worker Herod expected to see! His face was already badly bruised and swollen from the abuse He had taken. Spittle and blood were drying in His matted hair. Tired and physically weakened from a sleepless night, He stood before Herod, bound and under guard like a common criminal.[9]

2. As a woman, you have followed Jesus, donated money, listened to His teaching. What are you thinking when you see Him now? *Lord, I do not understand! You are our Savior & Lord, save us now.*

3. What does Herod hope for in Jesus (verse 8)?
He wanted to see him perform a miracle.

4. Why do you think Jesus answers Pilate but not Herod?
Jesus refused to perform as Herod expected for His amusement. Pilate saw through the Jewish leaders' ruse & wanted no part of it.

Read Luke 23:13–16 and Mark 15:6–14 (**Scene 10**).

Pilate still cannot find anything wrong with Jesus, and Pilate's wife even sends a note of warning (Matthew 27:19). Since a prisoner can be set free, Pilate offers to release Jesus. But the crowd prefers Barabbas, an insurrectionist and murderer. The cries of "Crucify him!" intensify. Pilate decides to *punish* Jesus. Maybe this will quench the crowd's cries for blood.

5. Pilate's wife has a dream. God has spoken to individuals in dreams before. Why is a woman's voice of reason inserted here, especially when her husband doesn't follow through?
To focus Pilate of Jesus' innocence.

Read Matthew 27:27–30 (**Scene 11**).

6. These four short verses are packed with details about Christ's torture.

Mark 15:19 adds that the soldiers fell on their knees and paid homage to Him; John 19:1 includes that Pilate took Jesus and had him flogged. A flogging can mean death itself. The *cat o' nine tails* had nine cords. Attached to the ends of the cords were lead balls, metal, or broken bones that gouged the skin. Jesus' hands are tied to a post. (The Jews restricted the flogging to thirty-nine lashes, but the *Romans* had no such rules. Jesus is flogged by *Romans*.[10])

> **Old Testament Prophecy Fulfilled:** "See, my servant will act wisely; he will be raised and lifted up and highly exalted." (Isaiah 52:13)
>
> "Just as Moses lifted up the snake in the desert, so the Son of Man must be lifted up." (John 3:14)

The Cross and the Shroud: A Medical Inquiry into the Crucifixion by Dr. Zugibe delves into the physical toll of flogging.

The bits of metal dug deep into the flesh, ripping small blood vessels, nerves, muscle, and skin. . . . The victim writhed and twisted in agony, falling to his knees, only to be jerked back on his feet time and time again until he could no longer stand up. Bouts of vomiting, tremors, seizures, and fainting fits occurred at varying intervals. . . . The victim was reduced to an exhausted, mangled mass of flesh with a craving for water. He was in a state of traumatic shock.[11]

Some believe the naked victim was shackled to a low column and bent over.[12] Others claim it involved a post and the wrists tied high, the body almost off the ground. If kidneys or certain arteries were wounded, the victim could die.[13] A flogging could expose veins, muscles, and sinews from the tops of the shoulders all the way to the backs of the legs[14] and because of the hematidrosis experienced in the Garden of Gethsemane, Jesus' skin would be extremely sensitive.[15]

The crown of thorns had two-inch long barbs.[16] Because of the sensitivity of the nerves, and the vascular nature of the scalp, Jesus experiences a spiking pain and much bleeding.[17] Dr. Zugibe writes,

They paid homage to the new king as they filed past, kneeling and then striking him across the face with the scepter and spitting on him. His cheeks and nose became reddened, bruised, and swollen, and stabbing pains that felt like electric shocks or red-hot pokers traversed his face, immobilizing him so he was afraid to turn lest the pain might reoccur. His face became distorted, and Jesus tensed his whole body so that he would not move, for every movement activated little trigger zones, bringing on agonizing attacks.[18]

Old Testament Prophecy Fulfilled: "I offered my back to those who beat me, my cheeks to those who pulled out my beard; I did not hide my face from mocking and spitting." (Isaiah 50:6)

Mosaic Law

". . . but he must not give him more than forty lashes. If he is flogged more than that, your brother will be degraded in your eyes." (Deuteronomy 25:3)

During the flogging scene in Mel Gibson's *The Passion of the Christ,* I buried my head and plugged my ears. Later when I acted the part of Mary Magdalene in our local passion play, I recalled the movie scenes and uttered the words I had longed to scream, "STOP IT! STOP IT! STOP IT!"

But *should* we stop remembering what Jesus did for us?

📖 Read John 19:4–17 (**Scene 12**).

Pilate reveals a bloodied and beaten man, hoping to appease the crowd. When you see Him, do you long to sing?

O Sacred Head, now wounded, with grief and
*   shame weighed down,*
Now scornfully surrounded with thorns Thy only
*   crown;*
How art Thou pale with anguish, with sore abuse and scorn!

> **Old Testament Prophecy Fulfilled:** "Just as there were many who were appalled at him—his appearance was so disfigured beyond that of any man and his form marred beyond human likeness." (Isaiah 52:14)

7. Look at John 19:10–11 and record Pilate's three questions and Jesus' responses:

Pilate's question: **Jesus' Response:**

1. *Why don't you talk to me.* — *No answer*   *you have power*
2. *Don't you know that I have the power to release you or crucify you?*
3. *Where did you come from?*   *No answer*

After Pilate presents Jesus, he tries to wash his hands of all guilt. The crowd is willing to take on the consequences of their actions. Barabbas is released, and Jesus is led out. The soldiers mock Jesus and rip off the purple robe, which no doubt has stuck to His raw flesh. They return Jesus' clothes and lay a heavy cross on Him (Matthew 27:31).

📖 Read Luke 23:26–31, Mark 15:21–22 (**Scene 13**).

Jesus stumbles his way to Golgotha (skull), a public hanging site, carrying His own patibulum or crossbeam (or perhaps even a full cross), which could weigh anywhere from 30 to 110 pounds. He also may have worn a sign around His neck identifying His crime, much the same way the Passover lambs were marked as belonging to a certain family.[19] Combining the titles from the gospels resulted in this

> **Old Testament Prophecy Fulfilled:** "He was oppressed and afflicted, yet he did not open his mouth; he was led like a lamb to the slaughter, and as a sheep before her shearers is silent, so he did not open his mouth." (Isaiah 53:7)

"Green Tree" — If the innocent Jesus (green tree)
suffered at the hands of the Romans, what would
happen to the guilty Jews (dry tree).

label written in Greek, Latin, and Hebrew and posted above Jesus' head at Golgotha.[20]

THIS IS JESUS OF NAZARETH,
THE KING OF THE JEWS

Imagine if *you* were ordered to carry Christ's cross? One year in the passion play we lacked a Simon of Cyrene. Someone suggested that one of our Roman soldiers actually grab a spectator from the crowd. This spectator in street clothes forced all of us to consider ourselves Simon of Cyrene.

What about the women? Though it was dangerous to be associated with a condemned man, they follow, even crying publicly. Jesus stops for a moment and addresses their tears (Luke 23:28–30).

Jesus' Words in Action: The women are there on the Way of Sorrow. Jesus released them from the burden of demons, illnesses, and religious persecution, and now they know He will die on the cross. They have no idea what it will mean for their earthly and heavenly futures. They do not anticipate His resurrection. Have you ever felt you were on the Way of Sorrow? What can you learn from Jesus' suffering and His tender care for those following Him to His death?

> "Let us fix our eyes on Jesus, the author and perfecter of our faith, who for the joy set before him endured the cross, scorning its shame, and sat down at the right hand of the throne of God." (Hebrews 12:2)

There is so much to be learned from drawing near to the cross. Consider the rich hymn, "When I Survey the Wonderous Cross" below. Perhaps find a version on YouTube to worship with today.

"When I Survey the Wondrous Cross"

When I survey the wondrous cross on which the Prince
    of Glory died,
My richest gain I count but loss, and pour contempt on
    all my pride.
Forbid it, Lord, that I should boast, save in the cross of
    Christ, my God:
All the vain things that charm me most, I sacrifice them
    to his blood.
See, from his head, his hands, his feet, sorrow and love
    flow mingled down!
Did e'er such love and sorrow meet, or thorns compose
    so rich a crown?

Were the whole realm of nature mine, that were an
    offering far too small;
Love so amazing, so divine, demands my soul, my life,
    my all.

Wednesday: **Seven Last Words** *[handwritten: 9:00AM to noon]*

Each Gospel records at least twenty verses on the death of
Christ. Each writer highlights certain portions of that final day.
Place bookmarks in the following four locations to simplify
your study: Matthew 27:33, Mark 15:22, Luke 23:32, and John *[handwritten: Jesus carrying the cross by himself to Golgotha]*
19:17. *Timeline—The Clock ticks down . . . (Third hour) 9:00*
a.m. until noon: *[handwritten: Simon to Golgotha Golgotha 2 Criminals c Him]*

    Read Mark 15:23–28, Luke 23:32–34, and John
19:19–24. *[handwritten: Crucified soldiers threw deceit for His clothing]* *[handwritten: Father, forgive them. They do not know what they are doing.]*
The place of crucifixion was probably near Jerusalem's
North Wall (see map on p. 83) by a gate on a busy street so all
would know His "crime."[21] When Jesus arrives at Golgotha, the
soldiers tear off Jesus' clothes, which have become encrusted to
His bleeding back.[22] Though we usually see pictures of Him *[handwritten: Myrrh was an anesthetic. Jesus chose to fully endure the pain]*
in a loincloth, it is more likely He was stripped to nakedness.[23]

    1. What do we know about the specific crime of the other
two men crucified with Christ (Mark 15:27)?

[handwritten: They were revolutionaries.]

    2. What was Jesus offered to drink? Why do you think He
abstained (Mark 15:23)? *[handwritten: Wine c myrrh]*

    A mixture of vinegar and gall (a bitter myrrh
narcotic) is offered to help numb the pain. Jesus
does not receive it. He wants to be fully alert to
everything that happens.[24] Thus, when a sev-
en-inch nail, much like a railroad spike, is driven
into either the palm of His hand in the fold
near His thumb[25] or in His wrists, smashing His
median nerve, he experiences a terrible burning
pain.[26]

    The cross is raised, causing the weight of His
body to suddenly shift downwards, pulling his shoulders out of
joint. Over time, fluid will accumulate in his lungs and heart.[27]

> **Old Testament Prophecy Fulfilled:** "Dogs have surrounded me; a band of evil men has encircled me, they have pierced my hands and feet" (Psalms 22:16)

Though the Bible focuses more on the pain of Christ's crucifixion in the *Old* Testament rather than in the *New*, we now know much from research and reenactments. Jesus' mangled and scourged flesh scrapes against the rough wood of the cross; His muscles cramp; He feels the tremendous drag on his shoulder muscles and the unrelenting pain of His nail-pierced hands and feet. Sharp pains shoot through His thorn-imbedded scalp. Dehydrated, He experiences an unquenchable thirst. He be-comes nauseous and feverish. Jesus has been deprived of sleep, food, and water for quite some time.[28] And, oh, how He longs for the companionship of His Father.

In medical terms, He experiences hypovolemic shock (great blood loss), respiratory acidosis (acidic blood leading to irregular heartbeat), pericardial effusion (fluid around the heart), and pleural effusion (fluid on the lungs). The heart goes into overdrive; His blood pressure drops; kidneys fail, and He becomes thirsty from the loss of blood.[29] And yet, in the midst of that pain, He prays for his persecutors: "Father, forgive them, for they do not know what they are doing" (Luke 23:34).

3. We see Jesus live out His earlier words, "For if you forgive men when they sin against you, your heavenly Father will also forgive you" (Matthew 6:14). Given Jesus' witness and the way He forgives, is there any reason we *cannot* forgive? Is there someone you need to forgive today?

"Love your enemies and pray for those who persecute you, that you may be sons of your Father in heaven." (Matthew 5:44)

4. The sign over Jesus is written in Aramaic (a Semitic language with many similarities to Hebrew), Latin, and Greek. What is the conflict over the wording (John 19:19–22)? To this day, what is the difference between *saying* who Jesus is and just repeating who others say He is? *Others may say many things, but Jesus states clearly who he is.*

Jesus may own five pieces of clothing: sandals, robe, headpiece, belt and tunic. If a *quaternion* (squad of four) guards him, they'd each have one piece and need to gamble for the seamless tunic.[30] The soldiers cast lots, fulfilling the Old Testament prophecy, "They divide my garments among them and cast lots for my clothing" (Psalm 22:18).

As if the physical pain is not enough, Jesus is mocked. Soldiers, spectators and even the criminals taunt Him. Once again, Old Testament prophecy is fulfilled.

5. Read Matthew 27:39–44 and Luke 23:35–37. Then list the insults hurled at Christ. *You who are going to destroy the Temple & build it in 3 days, save yourself. Come down from the cross if you are the Son of God*

6. Which titles are incorrect. If they are correct, what is the problem? *Destroy the Temple – Jesus' body. Son of God – Jesus must fulfill God's plan. King of Israel – Jesus already worked*

> **Old Testament Prophecy Fulfilled:** "For he bore the sin of many, and made intercession for the transgressors." (Isaiah 53:12)
>
> *Son of God – mortal body many miracles & they did not believe.*

Jesus is crucified with criminals, one on each side. As the hours progress, each man makes a choice about the Son of Man. Just like today, each of us has a choice of whether to follow Jesus or not.

He saved others, but he cannot save himself. He's the King of Israel! Let him come down from the cross & we will believe in him. He trusts in God. Let God save him now if he wants him, for he said, "I am the Son of God"

7. In your own words rewrite the dialogue from Luke 23:39–43 as if it were a script.

CRIMINAL: *So you are the Son of God! Save us all. We are guilty. He is innocent.*
CRIMINAL: (*to other criminal*) *Aren't you afraid of God?*
CRIMINAL: (*to Jesus*) *Do not forget me when you go home to God*
JESUS: *I am holding a place for you.*

One woman responded to this question by saying that one criminal said, *"Get me down!"* while the other said, *"Take me up!"*

Jesus knows the heart of the criminal beside him. It matters not that the criminal has not been baptized, lived a sinless life, or spent a day in the synagogue. The man believes. Jesus came to die a criminal's death between criminals so that this man—and all else who believe—might have eternal life.

> "I tell you the truth, whoever hears my word and believes him who sent me has eternal life and will not be condemned; he has crossed over from death to life." (John 5:24)

Jesus spoke few words on the cross, but His words to the thief must have brought great assurance:

"I tell you the truth, today you will be with me in paradise" (Luke 23:43).

Jesus' Words in Action: I'm sure that Jesus put His Words into action and that He and the criminal next met in paradise. I would love to hear those words on my deathbed. I would love to hear the voice of Jesus confirm that I will spend eternity with Him in a place far better than earth. Can you say today with assurance that one day you will join Jesus in heaven? Jesus didn't want to pay the price for nothing.

Thursday: Near the Cross

In the hymn "Near the Cross," composer Fanny Crosby asked Jesus to keep her near the cross. Would it surprise you to know that she was blind? How poignant her request to "bring its scenes before me!" Indeed, may we, too, stand near the cross. And in our own spiritual blindness may we see the scenes from near the cross and be transformed by them.

> *Near the cross of Jesus stood his mother, his mother's sister, Mary the wife of Clopas, and Mary Magdalene. When Jesus saw his mother there, and the disciple whom he loved standing nearby, he said to her, "Woman, here is your son," and to the disciple, "Here is your mother." From that time on, this disciple took her into his home.*
> (John 19:25-27)

1. Where are the women standing? What does this signify? *Near the Cross. They had not abandoned him.*

2. How does Jesus look out for both John and Mary? Why does He select *John* to be a son to His mother?
   📖 Read John 19:25–27.

3. How does Jesus look out for both John and Mary? Why does He select *John* to be a son to His mother? *Jesus was the First born. It was his responsibility to care for her (m). His brothers were not there as far as we know. He loved John like a brother & trusted him to care for his mother.*

Old Testament Prophecy Fulfilled: "My strength is dried up like a potsherd, and my tongue sticks to the roof of my mouth; you lay me in the dust of death." (Psalm 22:15)

If John then took Mary away from the cross, that left Mary's sister, Mary the wife of Clopas, and Mary Magdalene. *Always Mary Magdalene.* As these women mourn for an enemy of Rome, they take a risk, especially by nearing the cross. These women could endure the same crucifixion for their loyalty.[31]

According to Matthew it is the sixth hour (using the Jewish system), or *noon* our time.[32] From the sixth until the ninth hour, the sky turns black. And at 3:00 p.m., Jesus cries out, "'*Eloi, Eloi, lama sabachthani?*' which means, 'My God, my *(Spoken in Aramaic).*

God, why have you forsaken me?'" (Matthew 27:46). endure the same crucifixion for their loyalty.[33]

Noon until 3:00 p.m.

📖 Read Matthew 27:45–50 and John 19:28–30.

4. What do those nearby think He is saying?
"He's calling Elijah."

Jesus is quoting the words from Psalm 22:1, "My God, my God, why have you forsaken me? Why are you so far from saving me, so far from the words of my groaning?" But Jesus doesn't need salvation. He would choose death even if He had to hammer Himself to the cross and hang one-handed.

Jesus has had no water for eighteen hours and lost much water. An exhausting evening of prayer in the garden was followed by sweating due to the pain of scourging and the crown of thorns, plus hauling the heavy cross.[34] John 19:28 comments, "Later, knowing that all was now completed, and so that the Scripture would be fulfilled, Jesus said, 'I am thirsty.'"

5. What is the dying man on the cross offered to drink (see Matthew 27:48; John 19:29)? *Wine vinegar c̄ myrrh (narcotic) To extend life + pain.*

The second liquid offered is a cheap, sour wine used to make the victim's life linger in extended pain.[35] According to John, what do they use to put this liquid to Jesus' lips? A hyssop plant. Do you remember what was used to spread the blood around the doorframe on the night of Passover? Hyssop.[36]

We are now down to Jesus' near-final three triumphant words. John 19:30 relates, "When he had received the drink, Jesus said, **'It is finished.'** With that, he bowed his head and gave up his spirit" (emphasis added).

He knows that His mission on earth is nearly completed, He has reached the finish line, and His love is greater than the pain. With every last ounce of strength, Jesus calls out in a loud voice, "'Father, into your hands I commit my spirit.' When he had said this, he breathed his last" (Luke 23:46).

The shofar is blown at 3 p.m., announcing the sacrifice of the lamb.[37]

At that moment the curtain of the temple was torn in two from top to bottom. The earth shook, the rocks split and the tombs broke open. The bodies of many holy people who had died were raised to life. They came out of the tombs after Jesus' resurrection and went into the holy city and appeared to many people. (Matthew 27:51–53)

6. Underline from the passage above all of the amazing things spectators witnessed that day.

Once a year, on the Day of Atonement, the high priest entered the Holy of Holies to offer the blood of a sacrifice behind a 19 x 60 foot veil, perhaps six inches thick.[38]

7. Who tears the temple curtain in half? Why does it need tearing? *God, giving man direct access to God.*

The answer to that question can be found in Hebrews 10:19–22,

Therefore, brothers, since we have confidence to enter the Most Holy Place by the blood of Jesus, by a new and living way opened for us through the curtain, that is, his body, and since we have a great priest over the house of God, let us draw near to God with a sincere heart in full assurance of faith, having our hearts sprinkled to cleanse us from a guilty conscience and having our bodies washed with pure water.

The old system of sacrifices is over, torn away. Now all can freely approach God.[39]

8. How do onlookers react to the strange happenings (see Matthew 27:54; Luke 23:47–49)? *Surely, He was the Son of God. Surely, this was a righteous man.*

There is a huge "BUT" in Luke 23:47–49. *Was he really the Son of God?*

9. In contrast to the other observers, what do the women do? What is going through their minds? Mark 15:40–41 reminds us which women remain at the cross.

📖 Read John 19:31–37. *They stood observing. They probably thought, "It is true what He told us." - Mary Magdalene, Mary the of James the (aunt) of Joseph ~ Salome.*

It is now Friday afternoon. The hours are counting down until the Sabbath. According to the Old Testament, Jesus' body must be taken off the cross (see Deuteronomy 21:23).

One way to speed someone's death during crucifixion is to break his legs. This either causes the victim to be unable to push his body upwards to gasp for air,[40] or deals the "final blow" resulting in deep shock, coma, and death.[41] After the soldiers take a mallet to the other two men's legs, they discover Jesus is already dead. To prove the death, a soldier pierces Jesus' side, releasing blood and water.

> *When you were dead in your sins and in the uncircumcision of your sinful nature, God made you alive with Christ. He forgave us all our sins, having canceled the written code, with its regulations, that was against us and that stood opposed to us; he took it away, nailing it to the cross.* (Colossians 2:13–14)

Jesus nailed our sins to the cross.

Friday: Part One: Journey to the Tomb

And then it's over. A dead body hangs on the cross. Now what? Who will take over?

Mary Magdalene & Mary the mother of Joseph saw where he was laid.

📖 Read Matthew 27:57–66 (also Mark 15:42–47; Luke 23:50–56; John 19:38–42).

1. Underline what we know about Joseph from the Scriptures below.

> *As evening approached, there came a rich man from Arimathea, named Joseph, who had himself become a disciple of Jesus....and placed it in his own new tomb that he had cut out of the rock. He rolled a big stone in front of the entrance to the tomb and went away.* (Matthew 27:57, 60)
>
> *Joseph of Arimathea, a prominent member of the Council, who was himself waiting for the kingdom of God, went boldly to Pilate and asked for Jesus' body.* (Mark 15:43)
>
> *. . . who had not consented to their decision and action. He came from the Judean town of Arimathea, and he himself was waiting for the kingdom of God.* (Luke 23:51)

> **Old Testament Prophecy Fulfilled:** "He was assigned a grave with the wicked, and with the rich in his death, though he had done no violence, nor was any deceit in his mouth." (Isaiah 53:9)

Joseph was part of the Sanhedrin.

John tells us that Joseph was a secret disciple of Jesus because he feared the Jews (John 19:38b). However, there's nothing secretive now. Joseph goes **boldly** to Pilate and asks for Jesus' body. This, too, fulfills prophecy.

Mark informs us Pilate is surprised Jesus is already dead. Pilate summons the centurion and asks if Jesus is dead. After the centurion confirms this, Pilate surrenders the body to Joseph (Mark 15:44–45). Do we need any more proof that Jesus is *dead*?

But brave Joseph does not act alone. John 19:39 records, "He was accompanied by Nicodemus, the man who earlier had visited Jesus at night." Nicodemus? You ask. That name rings a bell. Indeed. Nicodemus is the cowardly Pharisee who came under the cover of darkness to ask Jesus the most important question of Nicodemus' life. Today we're going to go back, and *way* back, to learn more about Jesus' teachings about eternal life.

📖 Read John 3:1–21.

2. Who is Nicodemus, and to what group does he belong? Why do you think he meets Jesus at night (verse 1)? *A member of the Jewish ruling council. The council planned to kill Jesus. Nicodemus could have been accused of disloyalty.*

Jesus' claims are bolder than Nicodemus' statement. Here is where we get that phrase "born again" (John 3:3). Nicodemus was confused. He's a literalist and asks, "How can a man be born when he is old? . . . Surely he cannot enter a second time into his mother's womb to be born!" (John 3:4).

3. List what Nicodemus learned about salvation from the following verses.

John 3:13	Son of Man came from heaven
John 3:14–15	Son of Man must be lifted up to bring eternal life.
John 3:16	*God gave His only son for our salvation*
John 3:17	*Jesus sent to save the world, not condemn*
John 3:18	*Those who believe in Him are not condemned.*
John 3:19	*Jesus was the light of the world to of darkness*
John 3:20	*Evil doers do not walk in the light.*
John 3:21	*Those who walk in the light walk in truth.*

Now Nicodemus comes out in broad daylight, bringing seventy-five pounds of myrrh and aloes to anoint the body of a crucified criminal. He and Joseph wrap the body in strips of clean linen cloth and spices according to Jewish burial customs (John 19:39b–40). The burial cloth is wrapped from Jesus' neck to his feet and then back up the front to His chest. Smaller strips follow.[42]

They place the body in Joseph's new tomb cut out of rock, which is believed by many to be located in the garden where Jesus was crucified (John 19:41). An ordinary person would be laid in the ground, not entombed in stone; this new tomb would have cost thousands of dollars in American money.[43]

Mary Magdalene and the other Mary have left the cross and followed Joseph and Nicodemus all the way to the tomb. Luke records,

> The women who had come with Jesus from Galilee followed Joseph and saw the tomb and how his body was laid in it. Then they went home and prepared spices and perfumes. But they rested on the Sabbath in obedience to the commandment. (Luke 23:55–56)

4. What concerns the Jewish leader (Matthew 27:62–64)?

They were afraid that Jesus' disciples would come & steal the body & tell people that he has been raised from the dead.

A cord is strung across the tombstone and glued down with wax or clay. The official seal of a "signet ring" is imprinted on the wax.[44] A squad (4–16 men) stands guard at the tomb.[45] A broken seal or opened grave meant death to the soldiers.[46]

Jesus' Words in Action: One of the most telling statements Jesus made to Nicodemus is recorded in John 3:16, the verse many of us memorize in our childhood. Nicodemus knew God loved Him so much he could come out of the darkness and into the light and have a relationship with His Savior. Indeed Nicodemus must have believed, for when the disciples failed their Savior, he joined Joseph to anoint Christ's body.

Put your name in the verse today: "For God so loved *Sandy* that he gave *Sandy* his one and only Son, that if *she* believes in him *she* shall not perish but have eternal life."

Friday: Part Two: Journey to the Tomb

Jesus is now dead and buried. This was a long day for your Savior. So much so that we have more to study. You may do it all on this day or spread it out over the weekend.

Think back to a time when you experienced a sudden and shocking loss. What happens after you learn of a tragedy? Quite often you enter a period of waiting. You feel numb; you sob; you can't sleep, and when you finally are able to sleep, it is interrupted, fitful sleep. You awaken to a vague and growing, gut-wrenching sorrow as you remember your loss. What do you do when your beloved is in the grave and you have no one to turn to? You can't fathom a lonely future without your beloved?

> "When the Sabbath was over, Mary Magdalene, Mary the mother of James, and Salome bought spices so that they might go to anoint Jesus' body." (Mark 16:1)
>
>

Jesus' female followers have just watched their Lord, friend, and Savior die a horrible death on a cross. The man who changed their lives is now dead, His body sealed in a tomb.

Though we have a sense of great anticipation for Resurrection Sunday, remember that Jesus' followers felt great sorrow and loss and didn't anticipate the "happily ever after" Easter ending.

What do you suppose Jesus' followers are asking or secretly wondering?

Is this it?

Is Jesus gone forever?

What do we do now?

The disciples cower; the women wait, and the rulers worry.

We don't read Jesus' followers counting down "Day 3, Day 2, Day 1. Ready, Set, GO FIND HIM!"

No, the only people even checking the tomb are the unbelievers worried the body will be stolen and the women who want to anoint the dead body. We see no resurrection hope or resurrection joy.

Put your bookmarks at Matthew 28, Mark 16, Luke 24, and John 20. We'll flip back and forth as we look at four accounts of resurrection Sunday. Once again, you may want to put the three passages up on your computer screen for easy reference.

The chronology of these passages is sometimes confusing. This only reinforces the accuracy of the story. Historian Paul

Maier writes, "And the fact that differences among them were not edited out or harmonized shows both the honesty of Early Church copyists and the fact that there was no agreed upon—and therefore partially fabricated—version."[47]

Today's study begins the day after the Sabbath.

📖 Read Matthew 28:1–7 and Mark 16:1–8.

Mary Magdaline, Mary (m) & James, & Salone

1. What words describe the angel? *An angel of the Lord; His countenance was like lightning & clothing white as snow*
— A young man clothed in a long, white robe.

2. What is the reaction of the guards? *Shook with fear of them & became like dead men.*
— No mention of guards.

3. Why do you think the women experience such fear? *They did not know what became of Jesus.*
— The guards could have charged them for being associated w Jesus

> "He is not here; he has risen! Remember how he told you, while he was still with you in Galilee: 'The Son of Man must be delivered into the hands of sinful men, be crucified and on the third day be raised again'" (Luke 24:6-7)

4. Who is first to hear the good news? What are their instructions? (Matthew 28:7; Mark 16:7)? *The women, tell the disciples & Peter. meet in Galilee.*

5. What do Matthew 28:8, Mark 16:8, Luke 24:1–8 say about the women's reactions? *Went quickly & fled the tomb, for they trembled & were amazed. They said nothing to anyone. They were afraid.*
— 2 men suddenly appeared in dazzling clothes
— they remembered what Jesus said? *✓they were terrified*

In AD 30, female witnesses are not admissible in court, suggesting that in a world where women are second-class citizens, men do not trust women to provide reliable information.

6. What will happen when they testify about what they've seen? *They will not be believed.*

📖 Read John 20:2–10.

7. Who do the women tell first, and what is the reaction? *They tell Peter that "They have taken the Lord's body out of the tomb & we don't know they have put him." Peter & John ran to the tomb. John first observed from outside.*

8. Describe the placement of the burial cloths (verse 7)?

The cloth that had covered Jesus' head was folded up & lying apart from the other wrappings.

The headpiece is folded, the strips of cloth just lying there. Paul Maier writes, "According to this literal interpretation of the Greek, in which John was written, it seemed as if the body simply vanished from its grave wrappings, leaving them exactly in place except for gravity flattening the main shroud."[48]

9. What exactly do the disciples believe? What do you believe? *They believed that he had risen from the dead.*

Jesus' Words in Action: A week before Easter, I took my daughters to see their adopted Grandma, Aunt Rae, who was dying of cancer. The girls and I had longed to say "goodbye" but had been prevented from visiting because of our various illnesses. Now Aunt Rae had just slipped into a deep sleep or coma. Nine-year-old Christine pulled out her violin and began playing a chorus by Handel as we all watched for any flicker of awareness.

When my daughter Christine finished, Christine turned back to us, and I saw tears streaming down her face. Christine had quietly sobbed while she played. My heart broke for her and for my seven-year-old daughter, Julia, who longed to say "I love you" once again.

But because of Easter, someday they will.

On the way home, we talked about how we would see Aunt Rae and talk to her again. She died before Easter and would spend a glorious resurrection day in heaven. We may not always get to say all our earthly goodbyes, but we look forward to an eternity of hellos.

> L*ove's redeeming work is done, Alleluia!*
>
> *"Christ the Lord is Risen Today" by Charles Wesley*

Paul Maier describes Easter as the only holiday that looks backwards as well as forwards in history. It's a festival that both recognizes the Passion and celebrates a future of glorious reunions.[49] Similarly, Philip Yancey echoes that Jesus' scars give him hope.

Because of Easter, I can hope that the tears we shed, the blows we receive, the emotional pain, the heartache over lost friends and loved ones, all these will become memories, like Jesus' scars. [Scars never completely go away, but neither do they hurt any longer.

We will have re-created bodies, a re-created heaven and earth. We will have a new start, an Easter start.[50] What gives you hope? What gives you a new Easter start? *Jesus' self-generation*

What seems dead in your life? What needs healing or reconciliation? The One who conquered death can bring life to a stale church, reconciliation to fractured relationships, and resurrected love to stale marriages.

In *The Power of a Praying Wife*, Stormie Omartian highlights Mary Magdalene's joy in discovering Jesus' resurrection. The joy of seeing something hopelessly dead brought to life is the greatest joy we can know. The power that resurrected Jesus is the very same power that will resurrect the dead places of your marriage and put life back into it. "God both raised up the Lord and will also raise us up by His power." (1 Corinthians 6:14)[51]

> *What gives you hope? What gives you a new Easter start? What needs healing or restoration?*

Works Cited

1. MacArthur, John, *The Murder of Jesus: A Study of How Jesus Died* (Nashville, TN: Thomas Nelson, 2000), 94.
Haidle, Helen, *Journey to the Cross: The Complete Easter Story for Young Readers* (Grand Rapids, MI: Zonderkidz, 2001), 93.
2. MacArthur, 110.
3. Ibid., 108.
4. Ibid., 162.
5. Haidle, 94; MacArthur, 104–105, 108.
6. Ibid., 115.
7. Ibid., 136.
8. MacArthur, 165.
9. Ibid., 176.
10. "Messiah in Passover," http://biblicalholidays.com.
Haidle, 117.
11. Zugibe, Frederick, *The Cross and the Shroud: A Medical Inquiry into the Crucifixion* (New York: Paragon House, 1988), 15–16.
12. Ibid., 15.
13. MacArthur, 183.
14. Strobel, Lee, *The Case for Christ: A Journalist's Personal Investigation of the Evidence for Jesus* (Grand Rapids, MI: Zondervan, 1998), 16.
15. Ibid., 14–15.
16. MacArthur, 192.
17. Zugibe, 24.
18. Ibid., 204.
19. "Messiah in Passover," http://biblicalholidays.com.

20. MacArthur, 203–204.

21. Ray Vander Laan and Focus on the Family Video (That the World May Know Series), *Faith Lessons on the Death and Resurrection of the Messiah: City of the Great King (2)* (Grand Rapids, MI: Zondervan, 1997, 1998), Volume 4, Video 1.

22. Zugibe, 45–46.

23. MacArthur, 202.

24. *The MacArthur Study Bible* (Nashville, TN: Thomas Nelson, Word Publishing, 1997), 1449.

25. Zugibe, 206–207.

26. "Messiah in Passover," http://biblicalholidays.com.
Strobel, 18.

27. Strobel, 19.

28. "Messiah in Passover," http://biblicalholidays.com.
Zugibe, 207.
MacArthur, 200.

29. Strobel, 20–21.

30. MacArthur, 202–203.

31. Ibid., 228.

32. Higgs, Liz Curtis, *Mad Mary: A Bad Girl from Magdala, Transformed at His Appearing* (Colorado Springs, CO: WaterBrook Press, 2001), 202.

33. Ibid.

34. Zugibe, 103.

35. *The MacArthur Study Bible,* 1625.

36. Bob Deffinbaugh, Th.M, "The Crucifixion (John 19:17–37)," http://www.bible.org.

37. Vander Laan and Focus on the Family Video (That the World May Know Series), *The True Easter Story: The Promise Kept* (Grand Rapids, MI: Zondervan, 2000).
Haidle, Helen, 154.

38. MacArthur, 231. (Miracles of Calvary Keathley)

39. Ibid., 231.

40. Ibid., 202, 239–240.

41. Zugibe, 84.

42. Haidle, 165.

43. Vander Laan and Focus on the Family Video, *The True Easter Story: The Promise Kept.*

44. Haidle, 166.

45. Ibid., 171.

46. Ibid., 178.

47. Maier, Paul L., *In the Fullness of Time: A Historian Looks at Christmas, Easter, and the Early Church* (Grand Rapids, MI: Kregel, 1991), 180–181.

48. Ibid., 185.

49. Ibid., 205.

50. Yancey, Philip, *The Jesus I Never Knew* (Grand Rapids, MI: Zondervan, 1995), 219.

51. Omartian, Stormie, *The Power of a Praying Wife* (Eugene, Oregon: Harvest House, 1997), 19.

Where Do We Go from Here?

Monday: Meeting the Risen Savior
Mary Magdalene Part II

Wouldn't you love to have a long talk with Mary Magdalene about those long hours after Jesus died? What was she thinking?

We know what she *does:* She visits the tomb. And because of her commitment to the man who saved her from hell on earth, she witnesses the glories of heaven. In a beautiful and tender reunion, she is the first to see Jesus after His resurrection.

📖 Read John 20:11–18.

1. What does Mary's answer reveal about what she thinks has happened to her Lord (verse 13)? *She has not fully understood the resurrection up to this time. Initially, she thought that His body had been stolen.*

2. What two questions does Jesus ask in verse 15? *Dear woman, why are you crying? Who are you looking for?*

3. What is the moment she realizes the gardener is actually Jesus? *When he speaks her name.*

His voice must be unforgettable for when Mary hears her name, she cries out in Aramaic, *"Rabboni,"* addressing Him as "Teacher."

Can you imagine when you hear Jesus say your name? The most tender greeting you've experienced will pale in comparison to the love saturated in Jesus' voice when he sees you at the beginning of eternity.

4. Jesus' next comment in John 20:17 indicates Mary's next reaction. How do you think Mary responded? *Mary does not want to lose Jesus again, but she is obedient, leaving with joy.*

A *woman* healed of seven demons is given the powerful news that Jesus has overcome Satan, the head of all demons, and has conquered death. A *woman* learns the news during a period of history when her testimony is considered invalid in most circles. And yet, Jesus tells Mary to go and tell![1]

Author Philip Yancey suggests if you're trying to build a case for the resurrection, you don't build it with unacceptable witnesses whose testimony will be questioned. But instead, the Gospel writers recorded the truth: women were the first witnesses of the resurrection.[2]

The Gospels agree on the primary facts. Mary Magdalene arrived at the tomb first, the tomb was open, the angels proclaimed the resurrection news, and Mary saw Jesus first.[3] Still, why did God give the most important news to inadmissible witnesses? I believe it's because of their commitment. Jesus honored those who followed Him every step of the way by revealing the greatest moment in history to them. Doesn't it make you want to take hold of Jesus' hand and not miss any part of the journey? What do we pass up if we're absent from the cross or the tomb?

📖 Read Matthew 28:8–11 and Luke 24:9–11. These verses describe Jesus' appearance to the women.

5. What is the reaction of the women (Matthew 28:8–10)? *Fear + joy. Clasped his feet + worshipped Him.*

> "When they heard that Jesus was alive and that she had seen him, they did not believe it." (Mark 16:11) ⚔︎✝︎

6. What is Jesus' instruction to the women (Matthew 28:10)? *Don't be afraid. Go + tell my brothers to leave for Galilee + they will see me there.*

7. What is the reaction of the eleven disciples (Luke 24:11)? *Initially, disbelief, thinking this was [im]possible. They go to investigate — all this, to be able to accept.*

28:10 calling the disciples, "brothers" indicates that he had forgiven them, even though they deserted + denied him.

8. Matthew 28:11 reveals that the word has gotten out to more than just the followers of Jesus. Who else knows? *The guards went into the city + told the leading priests what had happened.*

📖 Read Matthew 28:11–15.

9. What deception do the chief priests and elders devise? *They gave the guards a large bribe + were told to say that the disciples had stolen his body while they were asleep. The priests said that they would stand up for them if the governor found out. The story spread among the Jews who believe it today.*

Today there are many deceptive explanations for Jesus' alleged resurrection.

- ■ The women actually saw a gardener instead of the risen Lord.
- ■ The disciples moved the body.
- ■ Jesus was never really dead; he was merely "swooning."
- ■ The women and men were all seeing things.
- ■ Joseph moved the body to another place.
- ■ The women found the *wrong* empty tomb.
- ■ The gardener moved the body.
- ■ Romans stole the body.
- ■ Jews stole the body.
- ■ Jesus had a twin.

If Jesus never died, how does a badly damaged man get out of the grave with clothes plastered to His body, roll away a stone, walk miles on nail-pierced feet, and gain a following of cowering disciples?[4] And would those disciples actually risk their lives for a liar? Would the sheep who fled from their shepherd in the Garden of Gethsemane have the courage to stake *their* lives on the recreation of *His*? They're not even good enough actors to pretend He's resurrected!

Yes, the tomb has been unguarded from the time Joseph rolled the stone in front of the tomb until the time the soldiers secured it. But who would steal a dead body?[5] Nobody doubts that the body is *missing*; the question should be, "Where is the body?" The religious leaders only need to flaunt Jesus' body to end all the discussion and the growth of Christianity. And so their excuse that the disciples have *stolen* it further confirms that the tomb is *empty*.[6]

The truth is this: The tomb is empty because Jesus rose from the dead in the same body that was buried.[7] Whether we choose to accept it or not does not take away the simple truth that Jesus was born, lived, died, and rose again for all who believe, and the head that once was crowned with thorns is now crowned with glory!

Jesus' Words in Action: Did Jesus rise from the dead? If we answer "no," then we need to find answers to the following questions and more:

- ■ Why was the body unwrapped before it was stolen?
- ■ Why would guards leave their station?

- Why weren't the disciples punished for *stealing* the body?
- Why weren't the guards executed for allowing the body to be stolen?

There are simply too many questions that need to be answered if Jesus did not rise from the dead. He is the Resurrection and the Life. He said it (John 11:25). Believe it!

Tuesday: Sunday Afternoon with the Savior

Read Luke 24:13–29.

It's Sunday afternoon, and two men are walking the seven-mile journey *away* from Jerusalem to Emmaus (see map on p. 14). As they review the sad events of their weekend, they are downcast and miserable, obviously *not* awaiting any proof of the resurrection.

I once wrote a church sermon skit about the journey to Emmaus. In my skit's dialogue, when Jesus acts unaware about the headlines in Jerusalem, the two men are incredulous about His ignorance and question, "Where've you been? Under a rock or something?"

But in *Luke's* script they ask, "Are you only a visitor to Jerusalem and do not know the things that have happened there in these days?" (Luke 24:18). Indeed, Jesus is a *visitor* to earth. *Heaven* is His home, but He's hanging around to teach a few more lessons to make His resurrection real to many!

1. According to Luke 24:19, what do these two men know about Jesus? *That he was a man from Nazareth, a prophet who did powerful miracles, & a mighty teacher. Are you only a visitor to Jerusalem*

2. What do they hope Jesus will do (verse 21)? *They hoped that he had come to rescue Israel.*

3. In Week Five, we studied what the disciples were told by Jesus about His death and resurrection. The men on the walk to Emmaus tell their companion what they should recognize as the fulfillment of Jesus' prophecy. List the points below (verses 21–24). *The body was missing & the women testified that he was alive. 1) the body was gone*

4. Jesus must have been exasperated. The two are walking away from hope! But when do *we* know Jesus' promises and still walk away from them? Can you share a time when you've turned away from His extended arms?

When my marriage was troubled, I turned to the world, but he pursued me.

5. How does Jesus respond (v. 25-26)? *"You Foolish people! You find it so hard to believe all the prophets wrote in the scriptures. All this was predicted in the scriptures."*

6. What do His followers get to hear explained straight out of the mouth of Jesus (27)? *He teach them through the writings of Moses & all the prophets, explaining all the scriptures the things concerning himself.*

Wouldn't it be great to hear it from Jesus Himself? You can! The Word of God is still here for us to study, so we never walk away from hope!

📖 Read Luke 24:30–44.

7. What causes the men to see Jesus (verses 30–31)? *As he broke bread with them & gave it to them, their eyes were opened & recognized him.*

> "And beginning with Moses and all the Prophets, he explained to them what was said in all the Scriptures concerning himself." (Luke 24:27)

When Jesus breaks bread and gives thanks, something clicks. Their eyes are opened, they recognize Him, and poof—He disappears. They comment after their Sabbath of Sunday School stories and sermons, "Were not our hearts burning within us while he talked with us on the road and opened the Scriptures to us?" (Luke 24:32).

Indeed! I want to feel that same burning? Oh to walk and talk with Jesus!

8. Complete what they tell the eleven disciples and others gathered with them. "It is *true*! The *Lord* has *risen* and has *appeared* to Simon" (verse 34).

Can you imagine the joy of retelling the story of the journey, Jesus' prophecies, and revelations? And then as if to put an exclamation point at the end of the story, Jesus Himself appears and says, "Peace be with you" (verse 36).

9. How does Luke describe their emotions? Do they experience resurrection joy (verse 37)? *Frightened, thinking they were seeing a ghost.*

10. What does Jesus ask of them (Luke 24:39)? *Look at my hands & feet. Why are your hearts filled c doubt? Touch me.*

11. *Now* what is their reaction to Him (Luke 24:41)? *They stood in disbelief, filled c joy & wonder.*

12. In the midst of joy, amazement, and awe, I think it's humorous that Jesus asks if there is anything to eat. What a guy thing (Luke 24:41)! But why might Jesus have chosen that moment to dine? *He wanted to have communion c them to stir their memory, to let them know he was truly alive.*

The two men on the journey to Emmaus know Jesus' prophecy but walk *away* from hope. Sometimes when we are most distraught, we feel Jesus is no longer there. Each time I think of the journey of these two men, I remember my dear friends, Denny and Laura, who took another kind of journey to Emmaus.

> "This is what I told you while I was still with you: Everything must be fulfilled that is written about me in the Law of Moses, the Prophets and the Psalms."
> (Luke 24:44)

After repeated *in vitro* attempts and one miscarriage, Denny and Laura were told they were expecting a baby. They had high hopes and dreams for their child. Being strong musicians, they could imagine their child as an accomplished musician. They looked forward to providing a warm and nurturing home, only to discover that they were actually pregnant with twins, but one had died *in utero*. They later found out that the surviving baby was a girl with Down's Syndrome.

They were devastated. On the day Laura received the diagnosis, their daughter kicked for the first time. Laura is an inquisitive person, so she looked around the hospital cafeteria for anyone who might be in a similar situation. *Where do they hide all the Down's Syndrome kids?* she asked herself. She needed to talk.

Denny was cautious, distant, and angry. He wasn't sure this baby was meant to be. He had recently lost his father and his brother and now looked forward to a new family. He didn't want any more pain. Besides, this child might have a terrible life. And maybe this child would alter their marriage in ways he couldn't imagine. He was so weary with grief.

As the couple's days of crying turned to weeks of sadness and indecision, Laura attended a retreat on joy and began to hope she'd again feel joy. Though the two questioned, "Where is Jesus right now?" they slowly began to feel His gentle presence. They began to understand and relate to the two men on the journey to Emmaus who thought Jesus was far away when He was walking right there beside them.

Their daughter was born on January 18, 2000, a tiny, beautiful blonde-haired angel. Indeed, she altered their marriage and their lives in ways they couldn't imagine. Though their daughter has Down's Syndrome, she is healthy. Denny and Laura knew Jesus had journeyed with them through the nine months, so they gave their daughter a name that would forever remind them of His presence and joy. They named her *Emma and Us—Emmaus Joy.*

Laura likes to show off a picture of Emma at the age of two standing in front of a mirror in her flower girl dress (one of *three* weddings in which Emma was the flower girl!). Emma is admiring herself in her pretty dress. Standing behind her, also in the reflection, is the face of her father. That's the part Laura loves best. Denny was transformed. Oh, the love on Emma's Daddy's face! Emma Joy may not always fully grasp the depth of it, but her father's love and joy is mirrored there.

Jesus' Words in Action: Maybe you wonder if Jesus is on the journey with you. Perhaps you're even walking away from your Jerusalem and the hope of resurrection. Turn to the One whose love is mirrored in every look at you. And if you're afraid you just can't find the way, pray to God that the scales on your eyes will fall off. Ask Him to show you signs of spring and hope!

Wednesday: Side-by-Side with the Savior

Today let's look at a few more encounters with Jesus. When Jesus first appears to the disciples, Thomas is not with them. After the disciples give Thomas an update, he lives up to his "Doubting Thomas" moniker. Lest we be too hard on Thomas, let's remember that back when the other disciples reminded Jesus of the danger of returning to Jerusalem (John 11:8), Thomas said, "Let us also go, that we may die with him" (John 11:11).

Read John 20:24–29.

A week later the disciples convene, and Thomas is with them. Let's eavesdrop on their locked door session.

1. What does Jesus say to the disciples when He unexpectedly appears without opening a door (verse 26)?

Peace be with you.

2. Thomas doesn't say anything, but Jesus knows what Thomas needs in order to believe. What does Jesus say Thomas should do (verse 27)? *Put your fingers here, + look at my hands. Put your hand into the wound in my side. Don't be faithless any longer. Believe!*

> "Unless I see the nail marks in his hands and put my finger where the nails were, and put my hand into his side, I will not believe it." (John 20:25)

3. Do we know whether Thomas put his finger in Jesus' nail-pierced hands or reached out and put his hand in Jesus' side? What would it feel like to be Thomas and see the risen Lord and hear your own remark thrown back at you? *Shameful + sad for Thomas.*

4. There is only one response Thomas can make. Record it below (John 20:28). *"My Lord and my God!"*

5. Why are Jesus' words in John 20:27 and 29 for us as well? *We have not seen, but I/we are blessed because we believe in our spirits.*

6. Do we believe without seeing? Do you find yourself doubting and needing to hear Jesus' words, "Stop doubting and believe"? Consider the man in Mark 9:24 who begs Jesus, "I do believe; help me overcome my unbelief!" Remember, doubt is not the opposite of faith; disobedience is. Faith as small as a mustard seed is powerful.

7. Write a short prayer, asking God to help grow your faith (Matthew 17:20; Luke 17:6).

Jesus appears for a third time when the disciples are fishing. What joy the disciples must feel to have Jesus spend His day with them. I love the way John opens his story, "It happened this way. . . ."

Lord, I think that I have faith, even if it is small. I want to grow my faith through obedience. Guide me, Holy Spirit. In Jesus' name. Amen.

📖 Read John 21:1–14.

8. What does Jesus call them? (v. 5). *Fellows*

I'm not a fisherman, but I wonder, why would the fish choose one side over the other? I'm not sure I would obey his suggestion. Especially if I'm not sure who He is. Look at v. 7.

Peter impulsively puts his coat back on and jumps into the water, leaving the disciples to tow the net full of fish for the remaining hundred yards.

9. What does Peter do and why? *He put on his tunic, jumped from the boat & headed to shore. Maybe to confirm it was the Lord.*

10. What are some of the miraculous aspects of this catch (John 20:11)? *There were 153 large fish (the number of known types in the sea of Galilee — representing all men.) The net had not torn.*

Why do you think John notes in 21:12, "None of the disciples dared ask him, 'Who are you?' They knew it was the Lord." This scene closes with an even more intimate scene between drenched Peter and the Master he previously denied three times. *Helping Peter overcome his own doubts.*

📖 Read John 21:15–17 and fill in the chart. *Peter denied Jesus three times. Three times Jesus asked Peter if he loved him. It is one thing to say you love Jesus, but the real test is willingness to serve him. Peter had repented & Jesus*

Jesus' Question	Peter's Response	Jesus' Request (Actions)
Do you love me more than these?	Yea Lord, you know I love you.	Then feed my lambs.
Simon, son of John, do you love me?	Yes, Lord, you know I love you.	Then take care of my sheep.
Simon, son of John do you love me?	Lord you know everything you know that I love you.	Then feed my sheep.

is asking him to commit his life.

Jesus' Words in Action: Have you ever made critical mistakes like Thomas and Peter made? On Friday we'll look at Paul, a man who persecuted Christians in the early church. Jesus still used these three flawed men, because Jesus gives second, third, and fourth chances.

If you've doubted or denied Jesus and you want a fresh start, begin anew today. Jump into the water to rejoin the Lord and spend a breakfast with Him in prayer. Open the Word and ask for forgiveness and a fresh start. Jesus invites you to join Him for fellowship and a good walk on the beach. He has a plan for your life. Ask Him about it today.

Thursday: Ascension and the Gift of the Holy Spirit

Jesus has been with His followers for *forty* days. Forty is a number laden with historical significance. This number is attached to numerous biblical events, such as the duration of the flood (40 days and 40 nights), Jesus' fast in the wilderness (40 days), Elijah's stay on the mountain (40 days), and the number of years wandering in the desert. During this forty-day period following His resurrection, Jesus appeared at least twelve times and to at least five hundred people.[8] We've read that Jesus was seen, heard, touched, and, on at least four occasions, He ate with His friends.[9]

Luke describes this in Acts 1:1-4:

> *In my former book, Theophilus, I wrote about all that Jesus began to do and to teach until the day he was taken up to heaven, after giving instructions through the Holy Spirit to the apostles he had chosen. After his suffering, he presented himself to them and gave many convincing proofs that he was alive. He appeared to them over a period of forty days and spoke about the kingdom of God.*

📖 Read Matthew 28:16–20 below.

> *Then the eleven disciples went to Galilee, to the mountain where Jesus had told them to go. When they saw him, they worshiped him; but some doubted. Then Jesus came to them and said, "All authority in heaven and on earth has been given to me. Therefore go and make*

disciples of all nations, baptizing them in the name of the Father and of the Son and of the Holy Spirit, and teaching them to obey everything I have commanded you. And surely I am with you always, to the very end of the age."

1. Underline in the Scripture above what Jesus commands them to do.

2. Circle the concluding promise.

In Luke 24:45–50, Jesus tells them to "stay in the city until you have been clothed with power from on high." (v. 49).

In Acts 1:4-5 Luke writes,

Do not leave Jerusalem, but wait for the gift my Father promised, which you have heard me speak about. For John baptized with water, but in a few days you will be baptized with the Holy Spirit.

In Acts 1:6–11, Jesus is asked, "Lord, are you at this time going to restore the kingdom to Israel?" Do you wonder if Jesus is getting tired of that question. In part of His response, He tells them, "But you will receive power when the Holy Spirit comes on you; and you will be my witnesses in Jerusalem, and in all Judea and Samaria, and to the ends of the earth."

Their witness will encompass Jerusalem, extend to Judea and Samaria, and then to the "ends of the earth." If you draw a circle around Jerusalem, then a wider concentric circle including the provinces, and finally the whole world, you can see the visual picture Jesus was drawing.

Jesus would instruct me, "Go tell others about Jesus in Paeonian Springs, in Loudoun and Fairfax Counties, Virginia, West Virginia, the United States, and in the whole world." What are your instructions? Where could you witness about Christ's death and resurrection? And then the Ascension occurs and Jesus leaves for good until He returns at His Second Coming.

While he was blessing them, he left them and was taken up into heaven. Then they worshiped him and returned to Jerusalem with great joy. And they stayed continually at the temple, praising God. (Luke 24:51–53)

"50" is the number for Jubilee + a new start

After he said this, he was taken up before their very eyes, and a cloud hid him from their sight. They were looking intently up into the sky as he was going, when suddenly two men dressed in white stood beside them. "Men of Galilee," they said, "why do you stand here looking into the sky? This same Jesus, who has been taken from you into heaven, will come back in the same way you have seen him go into heaven." (Acts 1:9–11)

Jesus is coming back the same way He left. We have something big to prepare *for* and look forward *to*. His second coming will be a glorious event! Like the ten virgins, we need to have oil in our lamps and be ready for His return.

> "After the Lord Jesus had spoken to them, he was taken up into heaven and he sat at the right hand of God." (Mark 16:19)
>
>

The disciples couldn't just stand on the mountain and wait. So after worshiping Him, they "returned to Jerusalem with great joy." They "stayed continually at the temple, praising God," and the disciples and the women along with Mary, and Jesus' brothers "joined together constantly in prayer" (Luke 24:52–53; Acts 1:12–14).

Then we have Pentecost. Pentecost falls fifty days (*Pente = fifty*) after Passover and celebrates the harvest's first fruits. Jerusalem would have been crowded with visitors from around the world for this event. The gift of the Holy Spirit occurs at Pentecost. Let's see how Pentecost and the gift of the Holy Spirit intersect.

Read Acts 2:1–13:

When the day of Pentecost came, they were all together in one place. Suddenly a sound like the blowing of a violent wind came from heaven and filled the whole house where they were sitting. They saw what seemed to be tongues of fire that separated and came to rest on each of them. All of them were filled with the Holy Spirit and began to speak in other tongues as the Spirit enabled them. Now there were staying in Jerusalem God-fearing Jews from every nation under heaven. When they heard this sound, a crowd came together in bewilderment, because each one heard their own language being spoken. Utterly amazed, they asked: "Aren't all these who are speaking

Galileans? Then how is it that each of us hears them in our native language? Parthians, Medes and Elamites; residents of Mesopotamia, Judea and Cappadocia, Pontus and Asia, Phrygia and Pamphylia, Egypt and the parts of Libya near Cyrene; visitors from Rome (both Jews and converts to Judaism); Cretans and Arabs—we hear them declaring the wonders of God in our own tongues!" Amazed and perplexed, they asked one another, "What does this mean?" Some, however, made fun of them and said, "They have had too much wine."

Verse 1 indicates *"they were all together in one place."* This would include both men and women experiencing an amazing event.

"Many God-fearing Jews from every nation under heaven" (verse 5) are in Jerusalem at the time.

> "Therefore he is able to save completely those who come to God through him, because he always lives to intercede for them." (Hebrews 7:25)

3. How many regions are represented (verses 5, 9, 10–11)? *Jews from every nation, Parthians, Medes, Elamites, people from Mesopotamia, Judea, Cappadocia, Pontus & Asia, Phrygia, Pamphylia, Egypt and near (Cyrene), Rome, Cretes & Arabs*

4. Would you be surprised if I told you this event was also prophesied? Read on in Joel 2 below and underline what you see in the Old Testament about the gift of the Holy Spirit.

> *And afterward, <u>I will pour out my Spirit on all people. Your sons and daughters will prophesy, your old men will dream dreams, your young men will see visions.</u> Even on my servants, <u>both men and women,</u> I will pour out my Spirit in those days. <u>I will show wonders in the heavens and on the earth, blood and fire and billows of smoke</u> (Joel 2:28–30).*

This is another incident where Jesus fulfills prophecy and replaces old festivals with new celebrations. It is no accident that all Old Testament holidays are, or will be, replaced by Jesus. Jesus IS the celebration!

> "I am going to send you what my Father has promised; but stay in the city until you have been clothed with power from on high." (Luke 24:49)

Spring Festivals:	First Coming
Passover (Leviticus 23:4–8)	Lord's Supper (1 Corinthians 5:7–8)
Feast of Unleavened Bread	Crucifixion, Seed planted at beginning of Feast
Feast of First Fruits (Leviticus 23:11)	Resurrection – first fruits! (1 Corinthians 15:20, 23)
Feast of Weeks – 7 weeks harvest	Pentecost/Holy Spirit – 50 days
Fall Festivals:	**Second Coming**
Feast of Trumpets (Leviticus 23:23–24)	Jesus' Second Coming (1 Thessalonians 4:16–17)
Day of Atonement (Leviticus 23:26–28)	Judgment (Romans 3:23–25)
Feast of Tabernacles	Second Coming (Micah 4:1); Jesus lives among us

Jesus' Words in Action: Before Christ's death, He instructs His followers to be ready for His return by telling the Parable of the Ten Bridesmaids (see Matthew 25:1–13). We studied His comments about marriage at the Last Passover and in the garden. Though the women have lanterns, some are not prepared with enough oil for the bridegroom's return. He consistently describes His relationship to us as a marriage. As a woman how do you feel about being the bride of Christ and what does that teach you about Jesus? *He esteems women.*

Friday: The Holy Spirit in the Lives of Believers

120 believers were there.

I love a good "before and after" story complete with photographs. We've studied how Jesus changed the lives of many women and men. Today we'll see how the gift of the Holy Spirit does extreme makeovers on Christians in the early church.

After the gift of the Holy Spirit, Peter delivers a powerful sermon. Read Acts 2:22–36.

Peter has no doubts or fear, but what about his audience? They were "cut to the heart" and asked, "Brothers, what shall we do?" (Acts 2:37).

> "The Spirit and the bride say, 'Come!' And let him who hears say, 'Come!' Whoever is thirsty, let him come; and whoever wishes, let him take the free gift of the water of life." (Revelation 22:17)

📖 Read Acts 2:37–41.

1. Peter has the solution. What is his answer?

"*Repent* and be *baptized*, every one of you, in the name of *Jesus Christ* for the *forgiveness* of your *sins*. And you will receive the gift of the *Holy Spirit*. The promise is for you and your children and for all who are far off—for all whom the *Lord* our *God* will call." (Acts 2:38–39)

This sounds like Jesus' prophecy fulfilled. Jesus prophesied to the disciples before His ascension, telling them to stay in Jerusalem until they had been clothed with power from on high. After that they would preach repentance and forgiveness, beginning in Jerusalem (Luke 24:46–49). Three thousand were added to the faith that day.

Though the Sanhedrin doesn't like the growth of the church and imprisons and persecutes Christians, its members are timid about creating martyrs.[11] Peter is arrested, and the number of believers grows to five thousand (Acts 4:4). After being freed, Peter continues to expound with prophecy, finger pointing (Acts 4:10–11), and then concludes with the ultimate answer, "Salvation is found in no one else, for there is no other name under heaven given to men by which we must be saved" (Acts 4:12).

Could we be so bold? What is the ultimate reaction?

When they saw the courage of Peter and John and realized that they were unschooled, ordinary men, they were astonished and they took note that these men had been with Jesus. (Acts 4:13)

The Sanhedrin then asks, "What are we going to do with these men?" (Acts 4:16). Though they warn these men *not* to teach in the name of Jesus, Peter and John answer (my paraphrase), "No way! We're gonna preach Jesus! We can't *help* talking about what He has done!" (Acts 4:19–20).

How would a group with that kind of faith look as a community of believers? Let's find out in the next two passages.

> "You killed the author of life, but God raised him from the dead. We are witnesses of this." (Acts 3:15)

> **Jesus' Prophecy Fulfilled:** "I tell you the truth, unless a kernel of wheat falls to the ground and dies, it remains only a single seed. But if it dies, it produces many seeds." (John 12:24)

📖 Read Acts 2:42–47; 4:32–37.

2. List the many *bodybuilding* activities that bring Christians together in the early church. *Believers devoted themselves to the apostles teaching & fellowship; sharing meals (Lord's Supper) & to prayer. They shared everything they had.*

3. What would it be like to be a woman in this growing, sharing, grace-filled church with members who are one in heart and mind? *They had purpose, were valued & loved the Lord.*

> "All the believers were one in heart and mind. No one claimed that any of his possessions was his own, but they shared everything they had." (Acts 4:32)

Women are listed throughout the New Testament as they worship and serve in the early church. Perhaps in future study, you may want to read these accounts (Acts 1:14; 2:18; 5:14; 16:13–15, 40; 17:12; Romans 16:1–4, 6, 12, 13, 15).

Now note the emphasis on *both men and women*.

The early church grows with *both men and women* believers (Acts 5:14).

Both men and women are baptized (Acts 8:12).

Both men and women receive the Holy Spirit and prophesy in accordance with prophecy (Acts 2:18).

Both men and women of different backgrounds are taught. Prominent women, many of whom are Gentiles, are added to the church (Acts 17:4, 12), and now the apostles actually teach *women* (Acts 16:13). (Do you see a difference from your first week's study of women and religion?)

Both men and women of this early church are persecuted. *Both male and female* believers are dragged off and put in prison (Acts 8:3; 22:4).

📖 Read 1 Peter 1:6–9 below.

In all this you greatly rejoice, though now for a little while you may have had to suffer grief in all kinds of trials. These have come so that the proven genuineness of your faith—of greater worth than gold, which perishes even though refined by fire—may result in praise, glory and honor when Jesus Christ is revealed. Though you have not seen him, you love him; and even though you do not see him now, you believe in him and are filled with an inexpressible and glorious joy, for you are receiving the end result of your faith, the salvation of your souls.

Closing Thoughts
What does it all mean now?

The Cross

"For the message of the cross is foolishness to those who are perishing, but to us who are being saved it is the power of God." (1 Corinthians 1:18)

"May I never boast except in the cross of our Lord Jesus Christ, through which the world has been crucified to me, and I to the world." (Galatians 6:14)

"He himself bore our sins in his body on the tree, so that we might die to sins and live for righteousness; by his wounds you have been healed." (1 Peter 2:24)

4. What does the cross mean to *you?* After these eight weeks, what new thoughts have you gained about it? *Gal. 2:20 The cross is the sign of God's great mercy & grace; undeserved, but complete. If it were not for God the Jews, we as Christians would be lost.*

Jesus' Words in Action: Max Lucado writes, "The very instrument of the cross is symbolic, the vertical beam of holiness intersecting with the horizontal bar of love."[12]

5. Draw a picture of Lucado's words and place yourself beside the cross and write a prayer of thanks.

LOVE / holiness

Minister George Bennard answered his trials with a song. When he went through a difficult period, he considered the meaning of the cross and what it meant to share in Christ's suffering. After much study, reflection, and prayer, he wrote,

Lord, there are not sufficient words to express my finest gratitude for what You have done for me and fellow believers. May Your Holy name be praised forever more.

I saw the Christ of the cross as if I were seeing John 3:16 leave the printed page, take form and act out the meaning of redemption. The more I contemplated these truths the more convinced I became that the cross was far more than just a religious symbol but rather the very heart of the gospel.[13]

These reflections inspired the hymn "The Old Rugged Cross."

"The Old Rugged Cross"

On a hill far away stood an old rugged cross, the emblem of suff'ring and shame;

And I love that old cross where the dearest and best for a world of lost sinners was slain.

O that old rugged cross, so despised by the world, has a wondrous attraction for me;

For the dear Lamb of God left His glory above to bear it to dark Calvary.

To the old rugged cross I will ever be true, its shame and reproach gladly bear;

Then He'll call me some day to my home far away, where His glory forever I'll share.

So I'll cherish the old rugged cross, till my trophies at last I lay down;

I will cling to the old rugged cross, and exchange it some day for a crown.

The Blood

"In him we have redemption through his blood, the forgiveness of sins, in accordance with the riches of God's grace that he lavished on us with all wisdom and understanding." (Ephesians 1:7–8)

"How much more, then, will the blood of Christ, who through the eternal Spirit offered himself unblemished to God, cleanse our consciences from acts that lead to death, so that we may serve the living God!" (Hebrews 9:14)

"But if we walk in the light, as he is in the light, we have fellowship with one another, and the blood of Jesus, his Son, purifies us from all sin." (1 John 1:7)

"'Come now, let us reason together,' says the LORD. 'Though your sins are like scarlet, they shall be as white as snow; though they are red as crimson, they shall be like wool.'" (Isaiah 1:18)

6. What does the blood mean to you? What new thoughts have you gained about it? *The blood of the lamb covers my sins; past, present, & future. The blood protects me + have overcome death; just as the blood on the doorposts when the angel of death killed the Egyptian children.*

"Nothing but the Blood" was one of our VBS praise songs. Group Publishing took the simple gospel tune built on the first five notes of a scale and made it into a jammin' rap song. The kids especially loved it.

On Day 4 of VBS, the instructions were to sing the song a cappella. I began the solo "What can wash away my sins?" and waited for the children to respond.

It is a beautiful thing to hear one hundred children's voices sing the answer, "Nothing but the Blood of Jesus." For all the questions and statements below, there is but one answer: "Nothing but the blood of Jesus."

"Nothing but the Blood of Jesus"
What can wash away my sin?
What can make me whole again?
For my pardon this I see;
For my cleansing, this my plea
Nothing can for sin atone
Naught of good that I have done
This is all my hope and peace
This is all my righteousness

Chorus:
Oh! Precious is the flow that makes me white as snow
*No other fount I know, **nothing but the blood of Jesus***

Discipleship

Then Jesus said to his disciples, "If anyone would come after me, he must deny himself and take up his cross and follow me. For whoever wants to save his life will lose it, but whoever loses his life for me will find it. What good will it be for a man if he gains the whole world, yet forfeits his soul? Or what can a man give in exchange for his soul?" (Matthew 16:24–26)

Now if we are children, then we are heirs—heirs of God and co-heirs with Christ, if indeed we share in his sufferings in order that we may also share in his glory. I consider that our present sufferings are not worth comparing with the glory that will be revealed in us. (Romans 8:17–18)

7. What does it mean to be a follower of Christ? What does it mean to share in His sufferings? *Love one another as God has loved us with love beyond measure. I must not shy away from the hard stuff. My sufferings dull in comparison to what he did for me.* Perhaps the hymn "I Have Decided to Follow Jesus" sums it up well.

> *I have decided to follow Jesus*
> *No turning back, no turning back.*
> *Though none go with me, I still will follow*
> *No turning back, no turning back.*
> *The world behind me, the cross before me*
> *No turning back, no turning back.*

The words to this hymn would make a wonderful illustration. That's a souvenir picture you could draw in the margin as a reminder of what you've experienced these eight weeks.

I loved taking this journey with you. I may never meet you on earth, but one day our journey on earth will conclude with a glorious reunion in heaven!

In the meantime, remember, you are a woman created by God, loved by God and encouraged by Him to grow in relationship with Him. Follow Him, walk with Him, and look forward to the day—like the women of the New Testament—you will meet Jesus face to face. *I can only imagine*

"But rejoice that you participate in the sufferings of Christ, so that you may be overjoyed when his glory is revealed." (1 Peter 4:13)

Works Cited

1. Richards, Sue and Larry, *Every Woman in the Bible* (Nashville, TN: Thomas Nelson, 1999), 162.

2. Yancey, Philip, *The Jesus I Never Knew* (Grand Rapids, MI: Zondervan, 1995), 212.

Maier, Paul L., *In the Fullness of Time: A Historian Looks at Christmas, Easter, and the Early Church* (Grand Rapids, MI: Kregel, 1991,) 184.

3. Higgs, Liz Curtis, *Mad Mary: A Bad Girl from Magdala, Transformed at His Appearing* (Colorado Springs, CO: WaterBrook Press, 2001), 260.

4. Strobel, Lee, *The Case for Easter: A Journalist Investigates the Evidence for the Resurrection* (Grand Rapids, MI: Zondervan, 1998), 25.

5. Haidle, Helen, *Journey to the Cross: The Complete Easter Story for Young Readers* (Grand Rapids, MI: Zonderkidz, 2001), 183, Conclusion.

6. Maier, 198.

7. Geisler, Norman L., *The Battle for the Resurrection* (Nashville, TN: Thomas Nelson, 1989).

8. Maier, 188.

Strobel, *The Case for Christ: A Journalist's Personal Investigation of the Evidence for Jesus* (Grand Rapids, MI: Zondervan, 1998), 72.

Geisler, 141.

9. Geisler, 141.

10. Moore, Beth, *Beloved Disciple: The Life and Ministry of John* (Nashville, TN: LifeWay Press, 2002), 65–66.

"Overview of the Spring Holidays," http://biblicalholidays.com.

Ray Vander Laan and Focus on the Family Video, *The True Easter Story, That the World May Know* (Grand Rapids, MI: Zondervan, 2000).

11. *The Narrated Bible in Chronological Order*, F. LaGard Smith, (Eugene, Oregon: Harvest House, 1984), 1488

12. Morison, Frank, *Who Moved the Stone? A Skeptic Looks at the Death and Resurrection of Christ* (Grand Rapids, MI: Zondervan, 1930), 115.

13. Osbeck, Kenneth, *Amazing Grace 366 Inspiring Hymn Stories for Daily Devotions*, (Grand Rapids, Michigan: Kregel, 1990), 112.

Hymn Research:

Emurian, Ernest K., *Famous Stories of Inspiring Hymns* (Grand Rapids, MI: Kregel, 1956).

———, *Hymn Stories for Programs* (Grand Rapids, MI: Baker Book House, 1963).

Osbeck, Kenneth W., *Amazing Grace: 366 Inspiring Hymn Stories for Daily Devotions* (Grand Rapids, MI: Kregel, 1990).

———, *101 Hymn Stories: The Inspiring True Stories Behind 101 Favorite Hymns* (Grand Rapids, MI: Kregel, 1982).

Bailey, Albert Edward: *The Gospel in Hymns: Background and Interpretation* (New York: Charles Scribner's Sons: 1950).

Preparing My Heart for Easter

GUIDE FOR LEADERS

Other materials and resources to consider:

DVD: Ray Vander Laan's *The True Easter Story: The Promise Kept*. I strongly encourage the purchase of this inexpensive and beautiful video from Focus on the Family and That the World May Know Ministries. I also highly recommend any DVD in the "That the World May Know" video series. Check to see if your church library has this resource.

Handel's *Messiah* (Easter portion)

Easter music CD's

Devotions for Lent

Scenes from movies depicting the life, death, or resurrection of Jesus

The Visual Bible (http://www.visualbible.com): *Jesus The Christ, Matthew, Falling Fire*

Jesus, directed by Sykes, Kirsh.

See the endnotes for additional resources.

Other ideas

Consider charm bracelets with symbols for each week. Buying in bulk and online makes it affordable.

Consider a symbol per week to give to each woman (Rock, Cross, jar)

Preview—Conduct a meeting prior to Ash Wednesday

Discuss:

What do you remember about past Easters?

What made certain Easters more memorable?

What Easter resources do you use?

What would your ideal Easter be like?

How do you want this Easter to be different?

Pass out the study and introduce the format.

Read the Introduction together and point out the additional resources (maps p. 14, 66, Drama of Passion 96-97).

Show: *The True Easter Story: The Promise Kept* (That the World May Know series)

Music: Play selections from Handel's *Messiah*—The Easter portion as members enter.

Connections: Ask members to sign an information sheet. Prepare a list of names, addresses, phone numbers and E-mails. Ask members to bring in their personal Easter resources to share.

WEEK ONE: PREPARING FOR THE JOURNEY

Discuss:

Each week select questions for your group and ask members to share questions, reflections, and new learning.

1. Why is Easter sometimes given less importance than Christmas?
2. How could Easter be much more?
3. How have you celebrated the Lenten season in the past?
4. How have members celebrated Ash Wednesday?
5. Who are you similar to in the list of women?
6. What would have attracted you to Jesus?
7. What surprised you about how Jesus included women in His storytelling?
8. What surprised you about women of AD 30?
9. What did you learn about "I AM" statements?
10. What comforts you from the Beatitudes?
11. What is it you look for in a king or leader?
12. How is it reassuring to know that Jesus is the Great I Am?

Show: *Life and Ministry of the Messiah—The Rabbi* (That the World May Know series)

Music: "Near the Cross," "Hallelujah What a Savior," "Tell Me the Stories of Jesus"

Connections: Pass out list of addresses. Pass out a 3 x 5 card to each woman and ask them to write down their hopes for spiritual growth this Easter. Take the cards and pray for the women. Contact each one of them with a note card.

Memorize: John 13:34 or John 14:6

WEEK TWO: TRAVELING WITH JESUS

Discuss:

1. What surprised you about women of AD 30?
2. When is your quiet time?" Re: "In the morning"
3. Any new understanding about women of the N.T.?
4. How are these encounters obviously not accidents?
5. How did Jesus meet you?
6. What is one "takeaway" you learned from Jesus' encounter with each of the women this week? (Mother-in-law, Samaritan, adulterous woman, widow)

Show: *Death and Resurrection: Piercing the Darkness* (That the World May Know series)

Music: "What Wondrous Love Is This?" "I am Thine O Lord"

Connections: Pass out 3x5 note cards and ask each woman to write down a current prayer request. Have the women exchange cards with one another and place their friend's card in their Bible to keep their person in prayer.

Memorize: John 7:38–39 or Psalm 34:18

WEEK THREE: TRAVELING WITH JESUS

Discuss:

1. What is one "takeaway" you learned from Jesus' encounter with each of the women this week?)

2. When you see a familiar story to "restudy," how do you approach it so it is fresh?

3. Which of these characters were unfamiliar to you?

4. Which of the characters were familiar but taught you something new?

Music: "And Can It Be That I Should Gain," "My Jesus I Love Thee"

Connections: Pass out 3x5 cards and ask each woman to put their name and contact information on it. Mix up the cards and pass them out so each woman has a person to contact over the next week through a cheerful uplifting phone call, e-mail, or snail mail.

Memorize: John 11:25–26; Romans 12:1–2

WEEK FOUR: TRAVELING WITH JESUS

Discuss:

1. Which of these women could you relate to: Mary and Martha, the Bent Woman, Salome.

2. In what ways are you similar to Mary and in what ways are you similar to Martha?

3. Salome might have been a Stage Mom, Drama Mama or Soccer Mom. How can we relate to her? What did she fail to grasp?

4. Were there any surprises in the Overview?

Show: *The True Easter Story: The Promise Kept* (That the World May Know series; if you did not show it at a preview meeting)

Music: "The Old Rugged Cross," "There is a Fountain Filled with Blood," "Nothing but the Blood"

Connections: Pass out 3x5 cards and ask each woman to write down a special verse from the past week's lesson. Swap cards with one another.

Memorize: Luke 9:23

WEEK FIVE: PASSION WEEK—
ENTERING JERUSALEM

Discuss:

1. What surprised you from this week's lesson?

2. How is God working in your life this Lenten season?

3. How will you celebrate Easter differently this year?

4. If you were in Jerusalem at the time, where would you be physically and spiritually?

5. What kind of leader are you looking for?

6. What surprised you about the Q and A sessions from Wednesday?

7. What do you learn about Jesus from the Widow's offering. If you researched any of the other lessons, what did you learn??

8. What does it mean to live out James 1:27?

9. What surprised you about Jesus' anger?

10. What connections did you find between the Old and New Testaments?

11. How are we like the disciples?

Show: *The True Easter Story—Lamb of God* (That the World May Know series)

Music: Songs from Palm Sunday, "You Are My All in All," "There Is a Redeemer"

Connections: Bring red construction paper hearts jaggedly cut or torn in half. Pass out one half of a heart to each woman and have her write down her name and a prayer request on that piece. Ask each woman to find the match to her broken heart. Discuss the women we've studied, how their hearts must have been breaking, and that Jesus mends broken hearts. Ask each member to contact her "match" during the week.

Memorize: Zechariah 9:9 or Psalm 118:22–23 or John 12:24–25

WEEK SIX: PASSION WEEK—
THE LAST DAYS

Options:

Hold a Passover service.

The leader could wash the feet of the women in the group.

Discuss:

1. What was significant about the Passover lamb?

2. How does the week's study influence your taking of the Lord's Supper?

3. How are you encouraged with the illustration of the Bride of Christ?

4. What encourages you about the Holy Spirit?

5. What can you take away about Love, Peace, and Joy from Jesus' final teachings?

6. What look does Jesus give you?

Show: *Death and Resurrection: The Weight of the World* (That the World May Know series)

Music: "How Beautiful," "Lamb of God"

Connections: Pass out a sheet of paper to each member, then go around the room and trace each member's foot on the sheet. Then ask each woman to write down an area where she needs to walk like Jesus and serve. Each member should take home their foot as a visual reminder to step out in loving service.

Memorize: Mark 10:45, or John 14:5–7, or John 16:33

WEEK SEVEN:
THE WAY OF SORROW

Triduum: Maundy Thursday, Good Friday, The Great Vigil

Options:

Consider the Ash Wednesday practice of marking the forehead with ashes. Ask each member to wipe off the mark and carry the inward remembrance that Jesus took away our sins.

Celebrate the Lord' Supper and wash one another's feet.

Read through the Last Words of Jesus and extinguish candles during the remembrance.

Read aloud scenes from Gethsemane to Golgotha

Discuss:

1. What does the Passion of Christ teach you about God?

2. Have you ever felt like Peter and denied Jesus?

3. Were you able to read what Jesus did for you?

4. What did you learn about the Last Words from the Cross.

5. What does Jesus' interaction with the criminals tell us about Him?

6. Have you been able to stay near the cross like the women? If so, what have you witnessed?

7. How are you encouraged by the women's faithfulness in death and how Jesus showed up for them in life?

Music: "O Sacred Head," "When I Survey the Wondrous Cross," "Hosanna, Loud Hosanna!"

Show: *Death and Resurrection—Roll Away the Stone* (That the World May Know series)

Connections: Pass out a rock and felt permanent marker to each woman. Ask her to write down a hope she has for her Christian walk, a longstanding prayer, or something she longs to see resurrected in her life. This is a paperweight and a reminder that no stone is too big for God.

Memorize: Galatians 6:14 or John 15:10–11 or John 5:24

Can you think of a time when you had mixed emotions about what God told you to do? How did you handle that?

WEEK EIGHT: WHERE DO WE GO FROM HERE?

Discuss:

1. How is it significant Jesus appeared to women?

2. How could it be that Jesus' friends journeyed with Him but failed to recognize Him? How are we similar?

3. Have you ever been a doubting Thomas?

4. The Promised Holy Spirit is given. What is the command to go with the Holy Spirit?

5. What role does the Holy Spirit play in your life?

6. What does the blood, the cross, and discipleship mean to you now?

7. What is your level of commitment to Jesus now? Why?

8. Using Week One's list of women at the beginning of our study and our journey, who do you now relate to most?

9. Where do we go from here? (group or personal studies) In what way has studying how Jesus changed the lives of women--changed yours?

Music: "Jesus Christ is Risen Today," "Christ the Lord is Risen Today"

Show: *Life and Ministry of Messiah—No Greater Love* (That the World May Know series)

Death and Resurrection—Power to the People (That the World May Know series)

Connections: Share answers to prayer you've experienced, and ask for additional prayer requests. Ask each member to continue praying for the others in the group.

Memorize: 1 Peter 2:24 or 1 John 1:7

When you purchase a Bible or book from **AMG Publishers, Living Ink Books,** or **God and Country Press,** you are helping to impact the world for Christ.

How? AMG Publishers and its imprints are ministries of **AMG International,** a Gospel-first global ministry that meets the deepest needs – spiritual and physical – while inspiring hope, restoring lives and transforming communities. Profits from the sale of AMG Publishers' books are poured into AMG International's worldwide ministry efforts.

For over 75 years, AMG International has leveraged the insights of local leaders and churches, who know their communities best to identify the right strategies to meet the deepest needs. AMG's methods include child and youth development, media evangelism, pastor training, church planting, medical care and disaster relief.

To learn more about AMG International and how you can partner with the ministry through your prayers and financial support, please visit **www.amginternational.org**.

AMG INTERNATIONAL | MEETING THE DEEPEST NEEDS

ECFA ACCREDITED
Enhancing Trust

CHARITY NAVIGATOR
★★★★
Four Star Charity